77 Thai Recipes for Home

By: Kelly Johnson

Table of Contents

- Pad Thai
- Green Curry Chicken
- Som Tum (Green Papaya Salad)
- Massaman Curry
- Pad Kra Pao (Basil Chicken)
- Panang Curry
- Pineapple Fried Rice
- Red Curry Shrimp
- Thai Fish Cakes (Tod Mun Pla)
- Tom mKha Gai (Chicken Coconut Soup)
- Drunken Noodles (Pad Kee Mao)
- Mango Sticky Rice
- Thai Iced Tea
- Larb (Minced Meat Salad)
- Pad See Ew
- Chicken Satay with Peanut Sauce
- Thai Spring Rolls
- Cashew Chicken
- Thai Basil Beef (Pad Gra Prow)
- Coconut Chicken Soup (Tom Kha Gai)
- Green Papaya Pad Thai
- Red Curry Beef
- Thai Pumpkin Curry
- Thai Peanut Noodles
- Thai Yellow Curry
- Pineapple Chicken Curry
- Thai Crab Fried Rice
- Fried Bananas with Coconut Ice Cream
- Thai Beef Salad (Yam Nua)
- Chicken and Galangal Soup (Tom Kha Gai)
- Pad Prik Khing (Stir-Fried Green Beans with Red Curry Paste)
- Thai Basil Fried Rice
- Thai Cucumber Salad
- Thai Grilled Chicken (Gai Yang)
- Pad Pak (Stir-Fried Vegetables)

- Coconut Mango Pudding
- Spicy Thai Noodle Soup (Kuay Tiew Tom Yum)
- Thai Shrimp and Glass Noodle Salad)
- Thai Chicken Lettuce Wraps
- Thai Red Curry Noddles
- Fried Tofu with Peanut Sauce
- Thai Sweet Chili Sauce
- Thai Pineapple Fried Quinoa
- Thai Basil Pork (Pad Kra Pao Moo)
- Thai Chili Garlic Prawns
- Thai Corn Fritters
- Tom Yum Fried Rice
- Thai Style Grilled Fish
- Thai Coconut Pancakes (Kanom Krok)
- Thai Green Curry Noodles
- Thai Eggplant Stir-Fry
- Thai Red Curry Chicken Satay
- Thai Glass Noodle Salad (Yum Woon Sen)
- Thai Cashew Tofu Stir-Fry
- Thai Style BBQ Pork Skewers
- Coconut Banana Fritters
- Thai Green Papaya Soup
- Thai Basil Chicken Meatballs
- Thai Spicy Beef Salad (Nam Tok Nua)
- Thai Iced Coffee
- Green Curry Tofu
- Thai Style Grilled Chicken Wings
- Pad Woon Sen (Stir-Fried Glass Noodles)
- Thai Red Curry Mussels
- Thai Pumpkin Custard (Sangkhaya Fakthong)
- Thai Mango Salad
- Chicken in Pandan Leaves (Gai Haw Bai Toey)
- Thai Style Beef Jerky (Neua Dad Diew)
- Thai Coconut Chicken Skewers
- Pad Fak Thong (Stir-Fried Pumpkin)
- Thai Rice Soup (Khao Tom)
- Thai Shrimp Pancakes
- Spicy Thai Pineapple Chicken
- Thai Coconut Tapioca Pudding
- Thai Basil Eggplant

- Grilled Thai Lemongrass Chicken

Pad Thai

Ingredients:

For the Sauce:

- 3 tablespoons tamarind paste
- 3 tablespoons fish sauce
- 2 tablespoons soy sauce
- 1 tablespoon sugar
- 1/2 teaspoon chili flakes (adjust to taste)

For the Pad Thai:

- 8 oz (about 225g) rice noodles
- 2 tablespoons vegetable oil
- 2 cloves garlic, minced
- 1 cup firm tofu, diced (or your choice of protein like shrimp, chicken, or beef)
- 2 eggs, lightly beaten
- 1 cup bean sprouts
- 2 green onions, sliced
- 1/4 cup crushed peanuts
- Lime wedges for serving
- Fresh cilantro for garnish

Instructions:

Prepare the Rice Noodles:
- Soak the rice noodles in warm water for about 30 minutes until they are pliable but still firm. Drain and set aside.

Make the Sauce:
- In a small bowl, mix together tamarind paste, fish sauce, soy sauce, sugar, and chili flakes. Set aside.

Stir-Fry:
- Heat vegetable oil in a wok or large skillet over medium-high heat. Add minced garlic and stir-fry for about 30 seconds until fragrant.

- Add tofu (or your choice of protein) and cook until browned and cooked through.
- Push the tofu to one side of the wok and pour the beaten eggs into the other side. Scramble the eggs until cooked.

Combine Ingredients:
- Add soaked and drained rice noodles to the wok. Pour the prepared sauce over the noodles and toss everything together to combine.

Finish:
- Add bean sprouts and sliced green onions. Continue to stir-fry for another 1-2 minutes until the noodles are well-coated with the sauce and the vegetables are slightly tender.

Serve:
- Transfer the Pad Thai to serving plates. Garnish with crushed peanuts and fresh cilantro. Serve with lime wedges on the side.

Enjoy your homemade Pad Thai! Adjust the spice level and ingredients to suit your taste preferences.

Green Curry Chicken

Ingredients:

For the Green Curry Paste:

- 2 green Thai bird's eye chilies (adjust for spice preference)
- 2 shallots, peeled and chopped
- 4 cloves garlic, peeled
- 1 stalk lemongrass, sliced (use only the bottom half)
- 1 thumb-sized piece of galangal, peeled and sliced
- 1 teaspoon ground coriander
- 1/2 teaspoon ground cumin
- 1/2 teaspoon shrimp paste (optional)
- Zest from 1 lime
- 1/4 cup fresh cilantro leaves and stems
- 2 kaffir lime leaves, finely chopped (optional)
- 1 tablespoon vegetable oil

For the Curry:

- 1.5 lbs (about 700g) boneless, skinless chicken thighs, cut into bite-sized pieces
- 2 tablespoons vegetable oil
- 1 can (14 oz) coconut milk
- 1 cup chicken broth
- 2 tablespoons green curry paste (adjust to taste)
- 1 tablespoon fish sauce
- 1 tablespoon palm sugar or brown sugar
- 1 red bell pepper, sliced
- 1 cup Thai eggplants, halved (or substitute with regular eggplants)
- Fresh Thai basil leaves, for garnish
- Cooked jasmine rice, for serving

Instructions:

    Prepare the Green Curry Paste:
- In a food processor, combine all the green curry paste ingredients and blend until you have a smooth, vibrant green paste. Set aside.

    Cook the Chicken:

- Heat vegetable oil in a large pot or wok over medium heat. Add the green curry paste and sauté for 1-2 minutes until fragrant.
- Add chicken pieces and cook until browned on all sides.

Add Coconut Milk and Broth:
- Pour in the coconut milk and chicken broth. Stir well to combine.

Season the Curry:
- Add fish sauce and palm sugar (or brown sugar) to the pot. Adjust the seasoning according to your taste.

Simmer:
- Bring the mixture to a simmer and let it cook for about 10 minutes, allowing the flavors to meld.

Add Vegetables:
- Add sliced red bell pepper and halved Thai eggplants to the curry. Simmer for an additional 10-15 minutes until the vegetables are tender and the chicken is fully cooked.

Finish and Serve:
- Stir in fresh Thai basil leaves just before serving. Serve the Green Curry Chicken over cooked jasmine rice.

Enjoy your homemade Green Curry Chicken with its aromatic and spicy flavors! Adjust the spice level and ingredients to suit your taste preferences.

Som Tum (Green Papaya Salad)

Ingredients:

For the Salad:

- 1 medium-sized green papaya, peeled and julienned
- 2 medium-sized tomatoes, cut into wedges
- 1 cup long beans, cut into 2-inch pieces
- 2-3 Thai bird's eye chilies, minced (adjust for spice preference)
- 2 cloves garlic, minced
- 1/4 cup roasted peanuts, coarsely chopped
- 1/4 cup dried shrimp (optional)
- 1-2 tablespoons fish sauce (adjust to taste)
- 1-2 tablespoons palm sugar or brown sugar (adjust to taste)
- Lime wedges for serving

For the Dressing:

- 2 tablespoons lime juice
- 1 tablespoon tamarind paste
- 1 tablespoon fish sauce
- 1 tablespoon palm sugar or brown sugar

Instructions:

Prepare the Papaya:
- Peel the green papaya and cut it into thin, julienned strips using a mandolin or a knife. Place the julienned papaya in a large mixing bowl.

Make the Dressing:
- In a small bowl, mix together lime juice, tamarind paste, fish sauce, and palm sugar. Stir until the sugar is dissolved.

Assemble the Salad:
- Add the sliced tomatoes, long beans, minced chilies, and minced garlic to the bowl with the papaya.

Add Dressing and Toss:
- Pour the dressing over the ingredients in the bowl. Toss everything together until the salad is well-coated with the dressing.

Adjust Seasoning:

- Taste the salad and adjust the flavor by adding more fish sauce or sugar if needed.

Add Peanuts and Dried Shrimp:
- Sprinkle coarsely chopped peanuts and dried shrimp (if using) over the salad. Toss again to combine.

Serve:
- Transfer the Som Tum to a serving plate and garnish with additional peanuts. Serve with lime wedges on the side.

Enjoy the delightful combination of textures and flavors in this Green Papaya Salad! Adjust the spice level and ingredients to suit your taste preferences.

Massaman Curry

Ingredients:

For the Massaman Curry Paste:

- 2-3 dried red chilies, soaked in hot water
- 1 tablespoon coriander seeds
- 1 teaspoon cumin seeds
- 1/2 teaspoon cardamom seeds
- 1/2 teaspoon cinnamon
- 1/2 teaspoon ground nutmeg
- 4 cloves garlic, minced
- 1 thumb-sized piece of galangal or ginger, peeled and chopped
- 2 stalks lemongrass, white parts only, sliced
- 2 shallots, chopped
- 3-4 Thai bird's eye chilies, minced (adjust for spice preference)
- 1 tablespoon shrimp paste (optional)
- 1 tablespoon vegetable oil

For the Curry:

- 1.5 lbs (about 700g) beef, cut into bite-sized pieces (or protein/vegetables of your choice)
- 1 can (14 oz) coconut milk
- 1 cup beef or vegetable broth
- 2-3 tablespoons Massaman Curry Paste (adjust to taste)
- 2 tablespoons tamarind paste
- 2 tablespoons fish sauce
- 1 tablespoon palm sugar or brown sugar
- 2 potatoes, peeled and cut into chunks
- 1 onion, sliced
- 1/2 cup roasted peanuts
- Fresh cilantro for garnish
- Cooked jasmine rice, for serving

Instructions:

Prepare the Massaman Curry Paste:

- In a dry pan, toast coriander seeds, cumin seeds, cardamom seeds, cinnamon, and nutmeg over medium heat until fragrant. Let them cool.
- In a food processor, blend soaked dried chilies, toasted spices, garlic, galangal, lemongrass, shallots, Thai chilies, and shrimp paste (if using) until a smooth paste forms.

Cook the Curry:
- Heat vegetable oil in a large pot over medium heat. Add 2-3 tablespoons of the Massaman Curry Paste and stir-fry for 1-2 minutes until fragrant.

Add Protein and Coconut Milk:
- Add the beef (or your chosen protein) to the pot and brown on all sides. Pour in the coconut milk and beef or vegetable broth.

Season the Curry:
- Stir in tamarind paste, fish sauce, and palm sugar. Mix well and bring the mixture to a simmer.

Add Vegetables:
- Add the potato chunks and sliced onion to the pot. Simmer for 20-25 minutes or until the potatoes are tender.

Finish and Serve:
- Stir in roasted peanuts and let the curry simmer for an additional 5 minutes. Adjust the seasoning if needed.
- Serve the Massaman Curry over cooked jasmine rice, garnished with fresh cilantro.

Enjoy the comforting and aromatic flavors of Massaman Curry! Adjust the spice level and ingredients to suit your taste preferences.

Pad Kra Pao (Basil Chicken)

Ingredients:

- 1 lb (about 450g) ground chicken (or thinly sliced chicken breast/thighs)
- 2 tablespoons vegetable oil
- 4 cloves garlic, minced
- 2-3 Thai bird's eye chilies, minced (adjust for spice preference)
- 1 cup fresh Thai basil leaves (or holy basil if available)
- 1 tablespoon oyster sauce
- 1 tablespoon soy sauce
- 1 teaspoon fish sauce
- 1 teaspoon sugar
- 1/4 cup chicken broth or water
- Fried or over-easy eggs for serving (optional)
- Cooked jasmine rice, for serving

Instructions:

Prepare Ingredients:
- If using ground chicken, set it aside. If using chicken breasts or thighs, slice them thinly against the grain. Mince garlic, and chop Thai bird's eye chilies.

Stir-Fry:
- Heat vegetable oil in a wok or large skillet over medium-high heat. Add minced garlic and chilies, and stir-fry for about 30 seconds until fragrant.

Cook Chicken:
- Add the ground chicken (or sliced chicken) to the wok. Break up the meat and cook until it's no longer pink.

Season:
- In a small bowl, mix oyster sauce, soy sauce, fish sauce, and sugar. Add this sauce to the chicken and stir well to combine.

Add Basil:
- Once the chicken is cooked, add fresh Thai basil leaves to the wok. Stir-fry for an additional 1-2 minutes until the basil is wilted and aromatic.

Moisten with Broth:
- Pour chicken broth or water into the wok to create a bit of sauce. Stir to combine and let it simmer for another minute.

Adjust Seasoning:

- Taste the dish and adjust the seasoning if needed. You can add more soy sauce, fish sauce, or sugar according to your taste.

Serve:
- Serve Pad Kra Pao over cooked jasmine rice. Optionally, top each serving with a fried or over-easy egg.

Enjoy this quick and savory Thai Basil Chicken! Adjust the spice level and ingredients to suit your taste preferences.

Panang Curry

Ingredients:

For the Panang Curry Paste:

- 2-3 dried red chilies, soaked in hot water
- 2 tablespoons roasted peanuts
- 2 tablespoons chopped shallots
- 3 cloves garlic
- 1 tablespoon chopped galangal
- 1 tablespoon chopped lemongrass (only the white part)
- 1 teaspoon ground coriander
- 1/2 teaspoon ground cumin
- 1/2 teaspoon shrimp paste (optional)
- 1 tablespoon vegetable oil

For the Curry:

- 1.5 lbs (about 700g) boneless, skinless chicken thighs, cut into bite-sized pieces
- 2 tablespoons vegetable oil
- 1 can (14 oz) coconut milk
- 2-3 tablespoons Panang Curry Paste (adjust to taste)
- 1 tablespoon fish sauce
- 1 tablespoon palm sugar or brown sugar
- 1 kaffir lime leaf, finely shredded (optional)
- Red chili slices and fresh basil leaves for garnish
- Cooked jasmine rice, for serving

Instructions:

Prepare the Panang Curry Paste:
- In a food processor, blend soaked dried chilies, roasted peanuts, shallots, garlic, galangal, lemongrass, ground coriander, ground cumin, and shrimp paste (if using) until you have a smooth paste.

Cook the Chicken:
- Heat vegetable oil in a large pot or wok over medium heat. Add 2-3 tablespoons of the Panang Curry Paste and stir-fry for 1-2 minutes until fragrant.

- Add the chicken pieces and brown them on all sides.

Add Coconut Milk:
- Pour in the coconut milk and bring the mixture to a simmer.

Season the Curry:
- Stir in fish sauce and palm sugar. Adjust the seasoning according to your taste.

Simmer:
- Let the curry simmer for about 15-20 minutes until the chicken is cooked through and the flavors meld.

Garnish:
- Add shredded kaffir lime leaf (if using) and stir. Remove from heat.

Serve:
- Serve Panang Curry over cooked jasmine rice. Garnish with red chili slices and fresh basil leaves.

Enjoy the creamy and aromatic goodness of Panang Curry! Adjust the spice level and ingredients to suit your taste preferences.

Pineapple Fried Rice

Ingredients:

- 2 cups cooked jasmine rice (preferably chilled)
- 1 cup pineapple, diced
- 1 cup cooked and diced chicken, shrimp, or tofu (optional)
- 1/2 cup cashews or peanuts, toasted
- 1/2 cup frozen peas, thawed
- 1/2 cup carrots, finely diced
- 1/2 cup bell peppers (assorted colors), diced
- 3 green onions, thinly sliced
- 3 cloves garlic, minced
- 2 eggs, lightly beaten
- 3 tablespoons soy sauce
- 1 tablespoon fish sauce (or soy sauce for a vegetarian version)
- 1 tablespoon curry powder
- 1 teaspoon sugar
- 2 tablespoons vegetable oil
- Fresh cilantro for garnish
- Lime wedges for serving

Instructions:

Prep Ingredients:
- Ensure all ingredients are chopped and ready before starting.

Cook the Rice:
- If you haven't done so already, cook the jasmine rice and let it cool. It's best to use chilled rice for fried rice.

Stir-Fry Aromatics:
- Heat vegetable oil in a large wok or skillet over medium-high heat. Add minced garlic and stir-fry for about 30 seconds until fragrant.

Add Protein (Optional):
- If using chicken, shrimp, or tofu, add it to the wok and stir-fry until cooked through.

Scramble Eggs:
- Push the protein to one side of the wok and pour the beaten eggs into the other side. Scramble the eggs until just set.

Combine Ingredients:
- Add diced pineapple, cooked rice, cashews or peanuts, peas, carrots, bell peppers, and green onions to the wok. Stir everything together.

Season the Fried Rice:
- In a small bowl, mix together soy sauce, fish sauce (or soy sauce), curry powder, and sugar. Pour the sauce over the rice mixture and toss to combine.

Finish and Garnish:
- Continue stir-frying for another 3-5 minutes until everything is heated through and well mixed. Adjust seasoning if needed.
- Garnish with fresh cilantro.

Serve:
- Serve Pineapple Fried Rice hot, garnished with additional fresh cilantro and lime wedges on the side.

Enjoy the sweet and savory goodness of Pineapple Fried Rice! Adjust the ingredients and spice level to suit your taste preferences.

Red Curry Shrimp

Ingredients:

- 1 lb (about 450g) large shrimp, peeled and deveined
- 1 can (14 oz) coconut milk
- 2-3 tablespoons red curry paste (adjust to taste)
- 1 tablespoon vegetable oil
- 1 red bell pepper, sliced
- 1 zucchini, sliced
- 1 cup snap peas, ends trimmed
- 1 tablespoon fish sauce
- 1 tablespoon soy sauce
- 1 tablespoon brown sugar
- 1 kaffir lime leaf, finely shredded (optional)
- Fresh basil leaves for garnish
- Cooked jasmine rice, for serving

Instructions:

Prepare Shrimp:
- If the shrimp are frozen, thaw them and pat them dry. If fresh, ensure they are cleaned and deveined.

Prepare Vegetables:
- Slice the red bell pepper, zucchini, and trim the ends of snap peas.

Cook Red Curry Paste:
- Heat vegetable oil in a large skillet or wok over medium-high heat. Add 2-3 tablespoons of red curry paste and stir-fry for 1-2 minutes until fragrant.

Add Coconut Milk:
- Pour in the coconut milk and bring it to a simmer, stirring to combine the curry paste with the coconut milk.

Add Vegetables:
- Add the sliced red bell pepper, zucchini, and snap peas to the simmering curry. Cook for about 5 minutes or until the vegetables are slightly tender.

Season the Curry:
- Stir in fish sauce, soy sauce, and brown sugar. Mix well and adjust the seasoning according to your taste.

Add Shrimp:

- Add the peeled and deveined shrimp to the curry. Cook for an additional 5 minutes or until the shrimp are opaque and cooked through.

Garnish:
- Add shredded kaffir lime leaf (if using) and stir. Remove from heat.

Serve:
- Serve Red Curry Shrimp over cooked jasmine rice. Garnish with fresh basil leaves.

Enjoy the delightful combination of succulent shrimp and aromatic red curry flavors!

Adjust the spice level and ingredients to suit your taste preferences.

Thai Fish Cakes (Tod Mun Pla)

Ingredients:

For the Fish Cakes:

- 1 lb (about 450g) white fish fillets (such as cod or tilapia), finely chopped or minced
- 1-2 tablespoons red curry paste
- 1 egg
- 2 tablespoons fish sauce
- 1 tablespoon sugar
- 1 tablespoon cornstarch
- 1 kaffir lime leaf, finely shredded (optional)
- 1/4 cup green beans, finely chopped
- 1/4 cup fresh cilantro, chopped
- Vegetable oil for frying

For the Cucumber Relish:

- 1/2 cucumber, thinly sliced
- 1 shallot, thinly sliced
- 1/4 cup white vinegar
- 1/4 cup water
- 2 tablespoons sugar
- 1/2 teaspoon salt
- 1 red chili, thinly sliced (optional)

Instructions:

Prepare the Fish Cakes:
- In a food processor, combine chopped fish, red curry paste, egg, fish sauce, sugar, and cornstarch. Blend until you have a smooth paste.

Add Aromatics:
- Transfer the fish mixture to a bowl and add shredded kaffir lime leaf, chopped green beans, and cilantro. Mix well to incorporate the aromatics.

Shape and Fry:

- Heat vegetable oil in a frying pan or skillet over medium-high heat. Shape the fish mixture into small patties or balls and carefully place them in the hot oil.

Fry Until Golden Brown:
- Fry the fish cakes for 3-4 minutes on each side or until they are golden brown and cooked through. Work in batches to avoid overcrowding the pan.

Drain Excess Oil:
- Once cooked, transfer the fish cakes to a plate lined with paper towels to drain excess oil.

Prepare the Cucumber Relish:
- In a small bowl, mix together sliced cucumber, sliced shallot, white vinegar, water, sugar, salt, and red chili (if using). Stir until the sugar dissolves. Let it sit for a few minutes.

Serve:
- Serve the Tod Mun Pla hot, accompanied by the cucumber relish.

Enjoy these flavorful Thai Fish Cakes with the refreshing cucumber relish! Adjust the spice level and ingredients to suit your taste preferences.

Tom Kha Gai (Chicken Coconut Soup)

Ingredients:

- 1 lb (about 450g) boneless, skinless chicken thighs, thinly sliced
- 2 cans (14 oz each) coconut milk
- 2 cups chicken broth
- 1-2 stalks lemongrass, bruised and cut into 2-inch pieces
- 3-4 slices galangal or ginger, thinly sliced
- 3-4 kaffir lime leaves, torn into pieces
- 200g oyster mushrooms, sliced
- 1-2 red bird's eye chilies, thinly sliced (adjust for spice preference)
- 1 medium-sized onion, thinly sliced
- 2 tablespoons fish sauce
- 1-2 tablespoons lime juice
- 1 teaspoon sugar
- Fresh cilantro leaves for garnish
- Thai bird's eye chilies, sliced (optional, for extra heat)
- Cooked jasmine rice, for serving

Instructions:

Prepare Ingredients:
- Slice the chicken thighs thinly. Bruise the lemongrass by pressing it with the back of a knife. Slice the galangal or ginger thinly. Tear the kaffir lime leaves.

Simmer Broth:
- In a large pot, combine coconut milk, chicken broth, lemongrass, galangal or ginger, and kaffir lime leaves. Bring the mixture to a gentle simmer over medium heat.

Add Chicken and Vegetables:
- Add the sliced chicken, sliced mushrooms, sliced chilies, and sliced onion to the pot. Let it simmer for about 10-15 minutes until the chicken is cooked through and the flavors meld.

Season the Soup:
- Stir in fish sauce, lime juice, and sugar. Adjust the seasoning according to your taste. If you prefer more spice, you can add extra sliced bird's eye chilies.

Remove Aromatics:

- Before serving, remove the lemongrass, galangal or ginger slices, and torn kaffir lime leaves from the soup.

Serve:
- Ladle the Tom Kha Gai into bowls. Garnish with fresh cilantro leaves.

Optional: Serve with Rice:
- Serve the soup on its own or with a side of cooked jasmine rice.

Enjoy the comforting and aromatic flavors of Tom Kha Gai! Adjust the spice level and ingredients to suit your taste preferences.

Drunken Noodles (Pad Kee Mao)

Ingredients:

- 8 oz (about 225g) wide rice noodles, cooked according to package instructions
- 2 tablespoons vegetable oil
- 3 cloves garlic, minced
- 2 Thai bird's eye chilies, minced (adjust for spice preference)
- 1/2 lb (about 225g) chicken, beef, shrimp, or tofu, thinly sliced
- 1 bell pepper, sliced
- 1 onion, sliced
- 1 cup Thai basil leaves, loosely packed
- 2 tablespoons oyster sauce
- 2 tablespoons soy sauce
- 1 tablespoon fish sauce
- 1 tablespoon sugar
- 1 tablespoon dark soy sauce (optional, for color)
- Lime wedges for serving

Instructions:

Prepare Rice Noodles:
- Cook the wide rice noodles according to the package instructions. Drain and set aside.

Stir-Fry:
- Heat vegetable oil in a wok or large skillet over medium-high heat. Add minced garlic and minced Thai bird's eye chilies. Stir-fry for about 30 seconds until fragrant.

Add Protein:
- Add the thinly sliced chicken, beef, shrimp, or tofu to the wok. Cook until the protein is browned and cooked through.

Add Vegetables:
- Add sliced bell pepper and onion to the wok. Stir-fry for another 2-3 minutes until the vegetables are tender-crisp.

Combine Sauce:
- In a small bowl, mix together oyster sauce, soy sauce, fish sauce, sugar, and dark soy sauce (if using).

Add Noodles and Sauce:

- Add the cooked rice noodles to the wok. Pour the sauce over the noodles and toss everything together to combine.

Add Thai Basil:
- Add Thai basil leaves to the wok and stir-fry for an additional 1-2 minutes until the basil is wilted and aromatic.

Adjust Seasoning:
- Taste the Drunken Noodles and adjust the seasoning if needed. You can add more soy sauce, fish sauce, or sugar according to your taste.

Serve:
- Serve the Drunken Noodles hot, garnished with lime wedges on the side.

Enjoy the bold and spicy flavors of Pad Kee Mao! Adjust the spice level and ingredients to suit your taste preferences.

Mango Sticky Rice

Ingredients:

For the Sticky Rice:

- 1 cup glutinous rice (also known as sweet rice)
- 1 cup coconut milk
- 1/2 cup sugar
- 1/2 teaspoon salt

For the Topping:

- 2 ripe mangoes, peeled, pitted, and sliced
- Sesame seeds for garnish (optional)

For the Coconut Sauce:

- 1 cup coconut milk
- 2 tablespoons sugar
- 1/4 teaspoon salt

Instructions:

    Soak the Sticky Rice:
- Rinse the glutinous rice under cold water until the water runs clear. Soak the rice in water for at least 4 hours or overnight.

    Steam the Rice:
- Drain the soaked rice. Place the rice in a steamer lined with cheesecloth or a clean kitchen towel. Steam the rice for 25-30 minutes or until it becomes tender and translucent.

    Prepare the Coconut Sauce:
- In a small saucepan, combine coconut milk, sugar, and salt for the coconut sauce. Heat over medium heat, stirring until the sugar dissolves. Set aside.

    Sweeten the Sticky Rice:
- In a separate saucepan, combine coconut milk, sugar, and salt for the sticky rice. Heat over medium heat until the sugar dissolves. Remove from heat.

    Mix Coconut Milk with Rice:

- Transfer the steamed sticky rice to a large bowl. Pour the sweetened coconut milk mixture over the rice. Mix well to coat the rice evenly. Let it sit for 15-20 minutes to allow the rice to absorb the coconut milk.

Serve:
- Spoon the sweetened sticky rice onto serving plates. Arrange sliced mangoes on top of the rice.

Drizzle with Coconut Sauce:
- Drizzle the coconut sauce over the mango and sticky rice.

Garnish:
- Garnish with sesame seeds if desired.

Enjoy:
- Serve Mango Sticky Rice warm and enjoy this delightful Thai dessert!

This dessert is not only delicious but also showcases the perfect balance of sweetness and creaminess from the coconut milk, paired with the natural sweetness of ripe mangoes. Adjust the sweetness and toppings according to your preference.

Thai Iced Tea

Ingredients:

- 4-5 Thai tea bags (or black tea bags)
- 4 cups water
- 1/2 cup sweetened condensed milk
- Ice cubes

Instructions:

Brew the Tea:
- Bring 4 cups of water to a boil. Add the Thai tea bags to the boiling water and let them steep for 5-7 minutes. If using black tea bags, adjust the steeping time according to the package instructions.

Strain the Tea:
- Once the tea has steeped, remove the tea bags, squeezing out any excess liquid. If you want a smoother texture, you can strain the tea through a fine mesh sieve or cheesecloth.

Sweeten with Condensed Milk:
- While the tea is still hot, add sweetened condensed milk to the brewed tea. Start with 1/2 cup and adjust the sweetness to your liking. Stir well until the condensed milk is fully dissolved.

Cool the Tea:
- Allow the sweetened tea to cool to room temperature. You can refrigerate it for faster cooling.

Serve Over Ice:
- Fill glasses with ice cubes. Pour the cooled Thai tea over the ice.

Optional: Garnish (Optional):
- Garnish the Thai Iced Tea with a slice of lime or a sprig of mint for extra freshness.

Enjoy:
- Stir and enjoy your homemade Thai Iced Tea!

Note: Thai Iced Tea often has a strong and distinctive flavor due to the use of Thai tea leaves, which include spices like star anise and tamarind. You can find Thai tea leaves at Asian grocery stores or use regular black tea bags as an alternative.

Feel free to adjust the sweetness and the amount of condensed milk according to your taste preferences. Thai Iced Tea is a delightful treat, especially on a hot day!

Larb (Minced Meat Salad)

Ingredients:

For the Larb:

- 1 lb (about 450g) ground chicken
- 2 tablespoons vegetable oil
- 3 tablespoons finely chopped shallots
- 3 cloves garlic, minced
- 1-2 Thai bird's eye chilies, minced (adjust for spice preference)
- 2 tablespoons fish sauce
- 2 tablespoons lime juice
- 1 tablespoon sugar
- 1 tablespoon roasted rice powder (optional)*
- 2 green onions, thinly sliced
- Fresh cilantro and mint leaves for garnish

For the Roasted Rice Powder:

- 2 tablespoons glutinous rice (sticky rice)

For Serving:

- Lettuce leaves or cabbage leaves
- Fresh herbs (cilantro, mint, Thai basil)
- Sliced cucumber
- Sticky rice (optional)

Instructions:

Prepare Roasted Rice Powder (Optional):
- In a dry pan, toast glutinous rice over medium heat until golden brown. Allow it to cool, then grind it into a coarse powder using a mortar and pestle or a spice grinder.

Cook Ground Chicken:
- Heat vegetable oil in a skillet over medium-high heat. Add ground chicken and cook until browned and cooked through.

Add Aromatics:

- Add chopped shallots, minced garlic, and minced Thai bird's eye chilies to the cooked chicken. Stir-fry for a couple of minutes until the aromatics are fragrant.

Season the Larb:
- In a bowl, combine fish sauce, lime juice, sugar, and roasted rice powder (if using). Stir well to dissolve the sugar.

Mix and Toss:
- Pour the seasoning mixture over the cooked chicken. Toss the mixture well to coat the chicken evenly.

Add Fresh Ingredients:
- Add thinly sliced green onions to the larb mixture. Toss again to combine.

Garnish:
- Garnish the larb with fresh cilantro and mint leaves.

Serve:
- Serve the Chicken Larb with lettuce or cabbage leaves, fresh herbs, sliced cucumber, and sticky rice (if using).

Enjoy assembling your own Larb wraps with the fresh and flavorful ingredients! Adjust the spice level and ingredients according to your taste preferences.

Pad See Ew

Ingredients:

- 8 oz (about 225g) wide rice noodles
- 2 tablespoons vegetable oil
- 1 lb (about 450g) broccoli florets
- 2 eggs, lightly beaten
- 1 lb (about 450g) boneless chicken thighs, sliced thinly (or substitute with tofu or shrimp)
- 3 cloves garlic, minced
- 1 cup carrots, julienned
- 1 cup Chinese broccoli or regular broccoli, chopped
- 3 tablespoons soy sauce
- 1 tablespoon oyster sauce
- 1 tablespoon dark soy sauce
- 1 tablespoon fish sauce
- 1 tablespoon sugar
- White pepper to taste
- Green onions, chopped, for garnish

Instructions:

Prepare the Rice Noodles:
- Cook the wide rice noodles according to the package instructions. Drain and set aside.

Prepare the Sauce:
- In a small bowl, mix together soy sauce, oyster sauce, dark soy sauce, fish sauce, and sugar. Set aside.

Stir-Fry the Chicken (or Tofu/Shrimp):
- Heat 1 tablespoon of vegetable oil in a wok or large skillet over medium-high heat. Add the sliced chicken and cook until browned and cooked through. If using tofu or shrimp, cook until tofu is lightly browned or shrimp turns pink. Remove the protein from the pan and set aside.

Stir-Fry Vegetables:
- In the same wok or skillet, add another tablespoon of oil. Add minced garlic and stir-fry for about 30 seconds until fragrant. Add julienned

carrots, broccoli florets, and Chinese broccoli. Stir-fry until the vegetables are tender-crisp.

Add Eggs and Noodles:
- Push the vegetables to one side of the wok and pour the beaten eggs into the other side. Scramble the eggs until just set. Add the cooked rice noodles and the sauce. Toss everything together to combine.

Combine Ingredients:
- Add the cooked chicken (or tofu/shrimp) back into the wok. Stir-fry everything together until well combined and heated through.

Season and Garnish:
- Season with white pepper to taste. Garnish with chopped green onions.

Serve:
- Serve Pad See Ew hot, with additional soy sauce or chili flakes on the side if desired.

Enjoy the rich and savory flavors of Pad See Ew! Adjust the ingredients and seasonings according to your taste preferences.

Chicken Satay with Peanut Sauce

Ingredients:

For the Chicken Satay:

- 1.5 lbs (about 700g) boneless, skinless chicken thighs, cut into thin strips
- 1 tablespoon soy sauce
- 1 tablespoon fish sauce
- 1 tablespoon curry powder
- 1 tablespoon turmeric powder
- 1 tablespoon vegetable oil
- 1 tablespoon brown sugar
- Bamboo skewers, soaked in water for at least 30 minutes

For the Peanut Sauce:

- 1 cup creamy peanut butter
- 1/4 cup soy sauce
- 2 tablespoons brown sugar
- 2 tablespoons rice vinegar
- 1 tablespoon fish sauce
- 1 teaspoon sesame oil
- 1 clove garlic, minced
- 1 teaspoon grated ginger
- 1/2 cup coconut milk (full-fat)
- 1 tablespoon lime juice
- Water (as needed to thin the sauce)

Instructions:

Marinate Chicken:
- In a bowl, mix together soy sauce, fish sauce, curry powder, turmeric powder, vegetable oil, and brown sugar. Add the chicken strips to the marinade, ensuring they are well-coated. Marinate for at least 30 minutes or preferably longer for better flavor.

Thread Chicken onto Skewers:
- Preheat your grill or grill pan. Thread marinated chicken strips onto soaked bamboo skewers.

Grill Chicken:
- Grill the chicken skewers over medium-high heat for 4-5 minutes on each side or until fully cooked and slightly charred.

Prepare Peanut Sauce:
- In a saucepan over medium heat, combine peanut butter, soy sauce, brown sugar, rice vinegar, fish sauce, sesame oil, minced garlic, grated ginger, coconut milk, and lime juice. Stir continuously until well combined and heated through. If the sauce is too thick, you can thin it with a little water.

Serve:
- Arrange the grilled Chicken Satay on a platter and serve with the Peanut Sauce on the side or drizzled over the top.

Garnish (Optional):
- Garnish with chopped peanuts, cilantro, or lime wedges if desired.

Enjoy the delicious flavors of Chicken Satay with Peanut Sauce as a snack or appetizer! Adjust the spice level and ingredients according to your taste preferences.

Thai Spring Rolls

Ingredients:

For the Filling:

- 1 cup shredded cabbage
- 1 cup shredded carrots
- 1 cup bean sprouts
- 1 cup thinly sliced mushrooms
- 1 cup cooked and cooled vermicelli noodles
- 1/2 cup chopped green onions
- 2 tablespoons soy sauce
- 1 tablespoon oyster sauce (optional for a non-vegetarian version)
- 1 teaspoon sesame oil
- 1 teaspoon sugar
- 1/2 teaspoon white pepper
- 1/2 cup cooked and chopped shrimp or tofu (optional)

For Wrapping:

- Rice paper wrappers (spring roll wrappers)
- Warm water for soaking the wrappers

For Frying:

- Vegetable oil for deep frying

Dipping Sauce:

- 1/4 cup soy sauce
- 2 tablespoons rice vinegar
- 1 tablespoon sugar
- 1 teaspoon sesame oil
- Red pepper flakes or sliced red chili (optional, for heat)

Instructions:

Prepare the Filling:
- In a large bowl, combine shredded cabbage, shredded carrots, bean sprouts, sliced mushrooms, vermicelli noodles, chopped green onions, soy sauce, oyster sauce (if using), sesame oil, sugar, white pepper, and cooked shrimp or tofu (if using). Toss the ingredients until well combined.

Prepare Rice Paper Wrappers:
- Dip a rice paper wrapper into warm water for about 15-20 seconds until it becomes pliable. Place it on a clean, damp surface.

Fill and Roll:
- Spoon a portion of the filling onto the lower third of the rice paper wrapper. Fold the sides of the wrapper over the filling, then roll it tightly from the bottom to the top.

Seal the Edges:
- Seal the edges of the rice paper by brushing a little water along the seam.

Repeat:
- Repeat the process until all the filling is used.

Heat Oil:
- Heat vegetable oil in a deep fryer or a deep skillet to 350°F (180°C).

Fry Spring Rolls:
- Carefully place the spring rolls into the hot oil, a few at a time, and fry until golden brown and crispy (about 3-4 minutes).

Drain:
- Remove the spring rolls with a slotted spoon and place them on a paper towel-lined plate to drain excess oil.

Prepare Dipping Sauce:
- In a small bowl, mix soy sauce, rice vinegar, sugar, sesame oil, and red pepper flakes or sliced red chili (if using).

Serve:
- Serve the Thai Spring Rolls hot with the dipping sauce on the side.

Enjoy the crunchy and flavorful Thai Spring Rolls as an appetizer or snack! Customize the filling according to your preferences.

Cashew Chicken

Ingredients:

- 1.5 lbs (about 700g) boneless, skinless chicken thighs, cut into bite-sized pieces
- 1 cup unsalted cashews
- 1 red bell pepper, diced
- 1 yellow bell pepper, diced
- 1 cup snap peas, ends trimmed
- 3 tablespoons vegetable oil
- 3 cloves garlic, minced
- 1 tablespoon soy sauce
- 1 tablespoon oyster sauce
- 1 tablespoon fish sauce
- 1 tablespoon hoisin sauce
- 1 tablespoon sugar
- 1 teaspoon cornstarch
- 1/2 cup chicken broth
- Green onions, chopped, for garnish
- Cooked jasmine rice, for serving

Instructions:

Prepare the Sauce:
- In a bowl, mix together soy sauce, oyster sauce, fish sauce, hoisin sauce, sugar, cornstarch, and chicken broth. Set aside.

Stir-Fry Chicken:
- Heat vegetable oil in a wok or large skillet over medium-high heat. Add minced garlic and stir-fry for about 30 seconds until fragrant. Add chicken pieces and cook until browned and cooked through.

Add Vegetables and Cashews:
- Add diced red and yellow bell peppers, snap peas, and cashews to the wok. Stir-fry for an additional 2-3 minutes until the vegetables are crisp-tender.

Pour Sauce:
- Pour the prepared sauce over the chicken and vegetables in the wok. Stir well to coat everything evenly.

Simmer:

- Allow the mixture to simmer for a couple of minutes until the sauce thickens slightly and coats the ingredients.

Garnish:
- Garnish with chopped green onions.

Serve:
- Serve Cashew Chicken hot over cooked jasmine rice.

Enjoy the delicious combination of tender chicken, crunchy cashews, and vibrant vegetables in a savory sauce! Adjust the ingredients and seasonings according to your taste preferences.

Thai Basil Beef (Pad Gra Prow)

Ingredients:

- 1 lb (about 450g) ground beef
- 2 tablespoons vegetable oil
- 4 cloves garlic, minced
- 2 Thai bird's eye chilies, minced (adjust for spice preference)
- 1 bell pepper, sliced
- 1 onion, sliced
- 1 cup fresh Thai basil leaves
- 2 tablespoons oyster sauce
- 1 tablespoon soy sauce
- 1 tablespoon fish sauce
- 1 teaspoon sugar
- White pepper to taste
- Cooked jasmine rice, for serving
- Fried egg (optional), for serving

Instructions:

Cook Ground Beef:
- In a large wok or skillet, heat vegetable oil over medium-high heat. Add minced garlic and minced Thai bird's eye chilies. Stir-fry for about 30 seconds until fragrant.

Add Ground Beef:
- Add ground beef to the wok and cook until browned.

Add Vegetables:
- Add sliced bell pepper and sliced onion to the wok. Stir-fry for 2-3 minutes until the vegetables are tender-crisp.

Prepare Sauce:
- In a small bowl, mix together oyster sauce, soy sauce, fish sauce, and sugar.

Season with Sauce:
- Pour the sauce over the beef and vegetables. Stir well to combine.

Add Thai Basil:
- Add fresh Thai basil leaves to the wok. Stir-fry for an additional 1-2 minutes until the basil is wilted and aromatic.

Adjust Seasoning:

- Taste the dish and adjust the seasoning if needed. You can add more soy sauce, fish sauce, or sugar according to your taste.

Serve:
- Serve Thai Basil Beef hot over cooked jasmine rice. Top with a fried egg if desired.

Enjoy the bold and aromatic flavors of Thai Basil Beef! Adjust the spice level and ingredients according to your taste preferences.

Coconut Chicken Soup (Tom Kha Gai)

Ingredients:

For the Soup:

- 1 lb (about 450g) boneless, skinless chicken thighs, thinly sliced
- 2 cans (14 oz each) coconut milk
- 2 cups chicken broth
- 1-2 stalks lemongrass, bruised and cut into 2-inch pieces
- 3-4 slices galangal or ginger, thinly sliced
- 3-4 kaffir lime leaves, torn into pieces
- 200g oyster mushrooms, sliced
- 1-2 red bird's eye chilies, thinly sliced (adjust for spice preference)
- 1 medium-sized onion, thinly sliced
- 2 tablespoons fish sauce
- 1-2 tablespoons lime juice
- 1 teaspoon sugar
- Fresh cilantro leaves for garnish
- Thai bird's eye chilies, sliced (optional, for extra heat)
- Cooked jasmine rice, for serving

Instructions:

Prepare Ingredients:
- Slice the chicken thighs thinly. Bruise the lemongrass by pressing it with the back of a knife. Slice the galangal or ginger thinly. Tear the kaffir lime leaves.

Simmer Broth:
- In a large pot, combine coconut milk, chicken broth, lemongrass, galangal or ginger, and kaffir lime leaves. Bring the mixture to a gentle simmer over medium heat.

Add Chicken and Vegetables:
- Add the sliced chicken, sliced mushrooms, sliced chilies, and sliced onion to the pot. Let it simmer for about 10-15 minutes until the chicken is cooked through and the flavors meld.

Season the Soup:

- Stir in fish sauce, lime juice, and sugar. Adjust the seasoning according to your taste. If you prefer more spice, you can add extra sliced bird's eye chilies.

Remove Aromatics:
- Before serving, remove the lemongrass, galangal or ginger slices, and torn kaffir lime leaves from the soup.

Serve:
- Ladle the Tom Kha Gai into bowls. Garnish with fresh cilantro leaves.

Optional: Serve with Rice:
- Serve the soup on its own or with a side of cooked jasmine rice.

Enjoy the comforting and aromatic flavors of Tom Kha Gai! Adjust the spice level and ingredients according to your taste preferences.

Green Papaya Pad Thai

Ingredients:

For the Green Papaya "Noodles":

- 1 green papaya, peeled and julienned (or use a spiralizer for noodle-like strips)
- 1 carrot, julienned
- 1 cucumber, julienned

For the Pad Thai Sauce:

- 3 tablespoons tamarind paste
- 2 tablespoons fish sauce (or soy sauce for a vegetarian version)
- 1 tablespoon oyster sauce (optional for non-vegetarian version)
- 1 tablespoon sugar
- 1 teaspoon chili paste or sriracha (adjust to taste)

For the Pad Thai Toppings:

- 1 cup cooked and diced chicken, shrimp, or tofu (optional)
- 2 tablespoons vegetable oil
- 3 cloves garlic, minced
- 2 eggs, lightly beaten
- 1 cup bean sprouts
- 1/4 cup chopped green onions
- 1/4 cup chopped peanuts
- Lime wedges for serving

Instructions:

Prepare the Green Papaya "Noodles":
- Peel and julienne the green papaya, carrot, and cucumber. You can use a julienne peeler or a spiralizer for noodle-like strips.

Make the Pad Thai Sauce:
- In a small bowl, whisk together tamarind paste, fish sauce (or soy sauce), oyster sauce (if using), sugar, and chili paste. Adjust the taste according to your preferences.

Stir-Fry Toppings:

- In a wok or large skillet, heat 1 tablespoon of vegetable oil over medium-high heat. Add minced garlic and stir-fry for about 30 seconds until fragrant. If using chicken, shrimp, or tofu, add and cook until they are cooked through.

Add Green Papaya "Noodles":
- Push the cooked toppings to one side of the wok. Add another tablespoon of oil to the empty side and pour in the beaten eggs. Scramble the eggs until just set. Mix the eggs with the cooked toppings.

Toss in "Noodles" and Sauce:
- Add the julienned green papaya, carrot, and cucumber to the wok. Pour the Pad Thai sauce over the vegetables and toss everything together. Cook for 2-3 minutes until the vegetables are slightly softened.

Finish and Serve:
- Add bean sprouts and chopped green onions to the wok. Toss everything together until well combined.

Serve:
- Plate the Green Papaya Pad Thai and sprinkle chopped peanuts over the top. Serve with lime wedges on the side.

Enjoy this refreshing and vibrant Green Papaya Pad Thai! Adjust the spice level and ingredients according to your taste preferences.

Red Curry Beef

Ingredients:

- 1 lb (about 450g) beef sirloin or flank steak, thinly sliced
- 2 tablespoons red curry paste
- 1 can (14 oz) coconut milk
- 1 red bell pepper, sliced
- 1 yellow bell pepper, sliced
- 1 cup bamboo shoots, sliced (canned, drained)
- 1 cup snap peas, ends trimmed
- 1 tablespoon vegetable oil
- 2 tablespoons fish sauce
- 1 tablespoon soy sauce
- 1 tablespoon brown sugar
- 1 kaffir lime leaf, torn into pieces (optional)
- Thai basil leaves for garnish (optional)
- Cooked jasmine rice, for serving

Instructions:

Prepare the Beef:
- Thinly slice the beef into strips.

Stir-Fry the Beef:
- In a wok or large skillet, heat vegetable oil over medium-high heat. Add the sliced beef and stir-fry until browned. Remove the beef from the wok and set aside.

Prepare the Curry Sauce:
- In the same wok, add red curry paste and cook for about 1-2 minutes until fragrant. Slowly whisk in the coconut milk, ensuring the curry paste is well combined with the coconut milk.

Simmer the Sauce:
- Bring the coconut milk mixture to a gentle simmer. Add fish sauce, soy sauce, and brown sugar. Stir well to combine.

Add Vegetables:
- Add sliced red and yellow bell peppers, bamboo shoots, and snap peas to the curry sauce. Allow the vegetables to simmer in the sauce until they are tender-crisp.

Add Beef:

- Add the cooked beef back to the wok. Stir to coat the beef with the red curry sauce. If using kaffir lime leaf, add it to the wok.

Simmer and Garnish:
- Let the Red Curry Beef simmer for a few more minutes to allow the flavors to meld. If using Thai basil leaves, add them to the wok just before serving.

Serve:
- Serve Red Curry Beef hot over cooked jasmine rice.

Enjoy the rich and aromatic flavors of Red Curry Beef! Adjust the spice level and ingredients according to your taste preferences.

Thai Pumpkin Curry

Ingredients:

- 2 cups pumpkin, peeled and cut into bite-sized chunks
- 1 can (14 oz) coconut milk
- 2-3 tablespoons red curry paste
- 1 cup firm tofu, cubed (optional)
- 1 red bell pepper, sliced
- 1 onion, sliced
- 1 cup bamboo shoots, sliced (canned, drained)
- 1-2 tablespoons vegetable oil
- 2 tablespoons soy sauce (or tamari for a gluten-free option)
- 1 tablespoon brown sugar
- 1 tablespoon fish sauce (optional for non-vegetarian version)
- Thai basil leaves for garnish (optional)
- Cooked jasmine rice, for serving

Instructions:

Prepare the Pumpkin:
- Peel and cut the pumpkin into bite-sized chunks.

Stir-Fry Tofu (Optional):
- If using tofu, heat 1 tablespoon of vegetable oil in a wok or large skillet over medium-high heat. Add the cubed tofu and stir-fry until golden brown. Remove the tofu from the wok and set aside.

Prepare the Curry Base:
- In the same wok, add another tablespoon of oil. Add red curry paste and cook for 1-2 minutes until fragrant.

Add Coconut Milk:
- Slowly whisk in the coconut milk, ensuring the curry paste is well combined with the coconut milk.

Simmer the Sauce:
- Bring the coconut milk mixture to a gentle simmer. Add soy sauce, brown sugar, and fish sauce (if using). Stir well to combine.

Add Vegetables and Pumpkin:
- Add sliced red bell pepper, onion, bamboo shoots, and pumpkin chunks to the curry sauce. Let the vegetables simmer in the sauce until the pumpkin is tender.

Add Tofu (Optional):
- If using tofu, add the stir-fried tofu back to the wok and stir to coat it with the curry sauce.

Simmer and Garnish:
- Let the Thai Pumpkin Curry simmer for a few more minutes to allow the flavors to meld. If using Thai basil leaves, add them to the wok just before serving.

Serve:
- Serve Thai Pumpkin Curry hot over cooked jasmine rice.

Enjoy the warm and comforting flavors of Thai Pumpkin Curry! Adjust the spice level and ingredients according to your taste preferences.

Thai Peanut Noodles

Ingredients:

For the Noodles:

- 8 oz (about 225g) rice noodles (flat or thin)
- 2 tablespoons vegetable oil
- 2 cloves garlic, minced
- 1 cup broccoli florets
- 1 red bell pepper, thinly sliced
- 1 carrot, julienned
- 1 cup bean sprouts
- 3 green onions, sliced
- Chopped cilantro and crushed peanuts for garnish (optional)

For the Peanut Sauce:

- 1/3 cup creamy peanut butter
- 3 tablespoons soy sauce
- 2 tablespoons rice vinegar
- 2 tablespoons brown sugar
- 1 tablespoon sesame oil
- 1 teaspoon ginger, minced
- 1 clove garlic, minced
- 1-2 teaspoons Sriracha or chili paste (adjust to taste)
- 2-3 tablespoons water (to thin the sauce)

Instructions:

Cook the Noodles:
- Cook the rice noodles according to the package instructions. Drain and set aside.

Prepare the Peanut Sauce:
- In a bowl, whisk together peanut butter, soy sauce, rice vinegar, brown sugar, sesame oil, minced ginger, minced garlic, and Sriracha. Add water gradually to achieve your desired consistency. Set aside.

Stir-Fry Vegetables:

- In a large wok or skillet, heat vegetable oil over medium-high heat. Add minced garlic and stir for about 30 seconds until fragrant. Add broccoli, red bell pepper, and julienned carrot. Stir-fry for 3-4 minutes until the vegetables are slightly tender but still crisp.

Combine Noodles and Sauce:
- Add the cooked rice noodles to the wok along with the prepared peanut sauce. Toss everything together until the noodles are well-coated with the sauce and the vegetables are evenly distributed.

Add Bean Sprouts and Green Onions:
- Add bean sprouts and sliced green onions to the wok. Toss for an additional 1-2 minutes until the bean sprouts are just wilted.

Garnish:
- Garnish with chopped cilantro and crushed peanuts if desired.

Serve:
- Serve Thai Peanut Noodles hot, optionally garnished with extra cilantro and peanuts.

Enjoy the rich and nutty flavors of Thai Peanut Noodles! Adjust the spice level and ingredients according to your taste preferences.

Thai Yellow Curry

Ingredients:

For the Curry:

- 1.5 lbs (about 700g) chicken, beef, shrimp, or tofu, cut into bite-sized pieces
- 1 can (14 oz) coconut milk
- 2-3 tablespoons yellow curry paste
- 1 large potato, peeled and diced
- 1 carrot, sliced
- 1 onion, sliced
- 1 bell pepper, sliced
- 1 cup broccoli florets
- 2 tablespoons vegetable oil
- 1-2 tablespoons fish sauce (or soy sauce for a vegetarian version)
- 1 tablespoon brown sugar
- 1 kaffir lime leaf (optional)
- Fresh cilantro leaves for garnish (optional)
- Lime wedges for serving

Instructions:

Prepare Protein:
- If using chicken, beef, or shrimp, season the protein with a bit of salt and pepper.

Cook Protein:
- In a large pot or wok, heat vegetable oil over medium-high heat. Cook the protein until browned and cooked through. If using tofu, you can brown it in the pan or add it later without pre-cooking.

Prepare Yellow Curry:
- Add yellow curry paste to the pot and stir for about 1-2 minutes until fragrant.

Add Vegetables:
- Add diced potatoes, sliced carrots, sliced onion, bell pepper, and broccoli to the pot. Stir to coat the vegetables with the curry paste.

Pour Coconut Milk:
- Pour in the coconut milk and stir well to combine. If using kaffir lime leaf, add it to the pot.

Simmer:
- Bring the mixture to a simmer and let it cook until the vegetables are tender, and the flavors meld (about 15-20 minutes).

Season the Curry:
- Season the curry with fish sauce (or soy sauce for a vegetarian version) and brown sugar. Adjust the seasoning according to your taste.

Garnish:
- Garnish with fresh cilantro leaves if desired.

Serve:
- Serve Thai Yellow Curry hot over steamed jasmine rice. Add lime wedges on the side for squeezing over the curry.

Enjoy the comforting and aromatic flavors of Thai Yellow Curry! Adjust the spice level and ingredients according to your taste preferences.

Pineapple Chicken Curry

Ingredients:

- 1.5 lbs (about 700g) boneless, skinless chicken thighs, cut into bite-sized pieces
- 1 can (14 oz) coconut milk
- 1 cup fresh pineapple chunks
- 1 red bell pepper, sliced
- 1 onion, sliced
- 2 tablespoons red curry paste
- 2 tablespoons vegetable oil
- 2 tablespoons fish sauce (or soy sauce for a vegetarian version)
- 1 tablespoon brown sugar
- 1 kaffir lime leaf (optional)
- Fresh basil leaves for garnish (optional)
- Cooked jasmine rice, for serving

Instructions:

Prepare Chicken:
- Season chicken pieces with salt and pepper.

Cook Chicken:
- In a large pot or wok, heat vegetable oil over medium-high heat. Cook the chicken pieces until browned and cooked through. Remove from the pot and set aside.

Prepare Pineapple Chicken Curry:
- Add red curry paste to the pot and stir for about 1-2 minutes until fragrant.

Add Vegetables:
- Add sliced red bell pepper and onion to the pot. Stir to coat the vegetables with the curry paste.

Pour Coconut Milk:
- Pour in the coconut milk and stir well to combine. If using kaffir lime leaf, add it to the pot.

Simmer:
- Bring the mixture to a simmer and let it cook for about 5-7 minutes until the vegetables are slightly tender.

Add Chicken and Pineapple:

- Add the cooked chicken back to the pot along with fresh pineapple chunks. Stir to combine.

Season the Curry:
- Season the curry with fish sauce (or soy sauce for a vegetarian version) and brown sugar. Adjust the seasoning according to your taste.

Simmer Again:
- Let the Pineapple Chicken Curry simmer for an additional 5-10 minutes to allow the flavors to meld.

Garnish:
- Garnish with fresh basil leaves if desired.

Serve:
- Serve Pineapple Chicken Curry hot over cooked jasmine rice.

Enjoy the tropical and savory flavors of Pineapple Chicken Curry! Adjust the spice level and ingredients according to your taste preferences.

Thai Crab Fried Rice

Ingredients:

- 2 cups cooked jasmine rice (preferably chilled)
- 200g crab meat (fresh or canned), picked through for shells
- 2 eggs, lightly beaten
- 1 cup mixed vegetables (peas, carrots, corn), thawed if frozen
- 3 green onions, chopped
- 3 cloves garlic, minced
- 2 tablespoons vegetable oil
- 1 tablespoon fish sauce
- 1 tablespoon soy sauce
- 1 teaspoon oyster sauce
- 1/2 teaspoon sugar
- Lime wedges for serving
- Fresh cilantro for garnish (optional)

Instructions:

Prepare Ingredients:
- Ensure that all ingredients are prepared and ready to go.

Heat Wok or Skillet:
- Heat a wok or large skillet over medium-high heat.

Stir-Fry Crab Meat:
- Add 1 tablespoon of vegetable oil to the wok. Add minced garlic and stir-fry for about 30 seconds until fragrant. Add crab meat to the wok and stir-fry for 1-2 minutes until heated through. Remove the crab meat from the wok and set aside.

Cook Eggs:
- In the same wok, add the remaining tablespoon of vegetable oil. Pour the beaten eggs into the wok and scramble them until just set.

Add Vegetables:
- Add the mixed vegetables to the wok and stir-fry for a couple of minutes until they are heated through and slightly tender.

Add Rice:
- Add the chilled cooked jasmine rice to the wok. Break up any clumps and stir-fry the rice with the vegetables and eggs.

Combine Ingredients:
- Add the cooked crab meat back to the wok. Stir in fish sauce, soy sauce, oyster sauce, and sugar. Toss everything together until well combined.

Add Green Onions:
- Add chopped green onions to the wok and stir-fry for an additional minute.

Garnish and Serve:
- Garnish with fresh cilantro if desired. Serve Thai Crab Fried Rice hot with lime wedges on the side.

Enjoy the delicious and savory flavors of Thai Crab Fried Rice! Adjust the seasonings according to your taste preferences.

Fried Bananas with Coconut Ice Cream

Ingredients:

For Fried Bananas:

- 4 ripe bananas, peeled and sliced into halves or quarters
- 1 cup all-purpose flour
- 1/4 cup rice flour
- 1/4 cup cornstarch
- 1/4 teaspoon baking powder
- 1/4 teaspoon salt
- 1 cup cold water
- Vegetable oil for frying

For Coconut Ice Cream:

- Coconut ice cream (store-bought or homemade)
- Shredded coconut for garnish (optional)

For Topping:

- Honey or maple syrup for drizzling (optional)
- Sesame seeds for garnish (optional)

Instructions:

For Fried Bananas:

Prepare the Batter:
- In a bowl, whisk together all-purpose flour, rice flour, cornstarch, baking powder, and salt. Gradually add cold water and whisk until you have a smooth batter.

Heat Oil:
- Heat vegetable oil in a deep fryer or a deep skillet to 350°F (180°C).

Coat Bananas:
- Dip each banana slice into the batter, ensuring it's well-coated.

Fry Bananas:
- Carefully place the battered banana slices into the hot oil and fry until golden brown and crispy (about 2-3 minutes per side).

Drain Excess Oil:
- Remove the fried bananas from the oil and place them on a paper towel-lined plate to drain excess oil.

For Serving:

Assemble Dessert:
- Place a scoop of coconut ice cream on a serving plate.

Top with Fried Bananas:
- Arrange the fried bananas around or on top of the coconut ice cream.

Garnish:
- Drizzle honey or maple syrup over the fried bananas (if desired). Sprinkle sesame seeds and shredded coconut on top for added texture and flavor.

Serve:
- Serve immediately while the fried bananas are still warm and crispy.

Enjoy the delightful combination of warm Fried Bananas with the cool and creamy Coconut Ice Cream! It's a perfect balance of textures and flavors.

Thai Beef Salad (Yam Nua)

Ingredients:

For the Beef:

- 1 lb (about 450g) beef sirloin or flank steak
- 2 tablespoons soy sauce
- 2 tablespoons fish sauce
- 1 tablespoon oyster sauce (optional)
- 1 tablespoon vegetable oil
- 1 teaspoon sugar
- 1/2 teaspoon black pepper

For the Salad:

- 1 cup cherry tomatoes, halved
- 1 cucumber, thinly sliced
- 1 red onion, thinly sliced
- 1 cup mixed salad greens (lettuce, arugula, or watercress)
- 1/2 cup fresh cilantro leaves
- 1/4 cup fresh mint leaves
- 1/4 cup roasted peanuts, chopped

For the Dressing:

- 3 tablespoons lime juice
- 2 tablespoons fish sauce
- 1 tablespoon soy sauce
- 1 tablespoon brown sugar
- 1-2 Thai bird's eye chilies, minced (adjust for spice preference)
- 2 cloves garlic, minced

Instructions:

Marinate the Beef:
- In a bowl, mix together soy sauce, fish sauce, oyster sauce (if using), vegetable oil, sugar, and black pepper. Marinate the beef in this mixture for at least 30 minutes to allow the flavors to infuse.

Grill the Beef:

- Preheat a grill or grill pan over medium-high heat. Grill the marinated beef for 3-4 minutes per side or until cooked to your desired level of doneness. Allow the beef to rest for a few minutes before slicing it thinly against the grain.

Prepare the Dressing:
- In a small bowl, whisk together lime juice, fish sauce, soy sauce, brown sugar, minced Thai bird's eye chilies, and minced garlic. Adjust the seasoning to your taste.

Assemble the Salad:
- In a large bowl, combine cherry tomatoes, sliced cucumber, thinly sliced red onion, mixed salad greens, fresh cilantro leaves, and fresh mint leaves.

Add Grilled Beef:
- Add the sliced grilled beef to the salad.

Drizzle Dressing:
- Drizzle the dressing over the salad and toss everything together until well combined.

Garnish:
- Garnish the Thai Beef Salad with chopped roasted peanuts.

Serve:
- Serve the Thai Beef Salad immediately, offering additional dressing on the side if desired.

Enjoy the vibrant and flavorful Thai Beef Salad! Adjust the spice level and ingredients according to your taste preferences.

Chicken and Galangal Soup (Tom Kha Gai)

Ingredients:

- 1 lb (about 450g) boneless, skinless chicken thighs, thinly sliced
- 1 can (14 oz) coconut milk
- 3 cups chicken broth
- 2 stalks lemongrass, bruised and cut into 2-inch pieces
- 4 slices galangal (or ginger), thinly sliced
- 3-4 kaffir lime leaves, torn into pieces
- 200g oyster mushrooms, sliced
- 1-2 Thai bird's eye chilies, thinly sliced (adjust for spice preference)
- 1 medium-sized onion, thinly sliced
- 2 tablespoons fish sauce
- 1-2 tablespoons lime juice
- 1 teaspoon sugar
- Fresh cilantro leaves for garnish
- Thai bird's eye chilies, sliced (optional, for extra heat)
- Cooked jasmine rice, for serving

Instructions:

Prepare Ingredients:
- Slice the chicken thighs thinly. Bruise the lemongrass by pressing it with the back of a knife. Slice the galangal or ginger thinly. Tear the kaffir lime leaves.

Simmer Broth:
- In a pot, combine coconut milk, chicken broth, lemongrass, galangal or ginger, and kaffir lime leaves. Bring the mixture to a gentle simmer over medium heat.

Add Chicken and Vegetables:
- Add sliced chicken, sliced mushrooms, sliced Thai bird's eye chilies, and sliced onion to the pot. Let it simmer for about 10-15 minutes until the chicken is cooked through and the flavors meld.

Season the Soup:
- Stir in fish sauce, lime juice, and sugar. Adjust the seasoning according to your taste. If you prefer more spice, you can add extra sliced bird's eye chilies.

Remove Aromatics:

- Before serving, remove the lemongrass, galangal or ginger slices, and torn kaffir lime leaves from the soup.

Serve:
- Ladle the Chicken and Galangal Soup into bowls. Garnish with fresh cilantro leaves.

Optional: Serve with Rice:
- Serve the soup on its own or with a side of cooked jasmine rice.

Enjoy the comforting and aromatic flavors of Chicken and Galangal Soup! Adjust the spice level and ingredients according to your taste preferences.

Pad Prik Khing (Stir-Fried Green Beans with Red Curry Paste)

Ingredients:

- 1 lb (about 450g) green beans, trimmed and cut into bite-sized pieces
- 1 lb (about 450g) chicken, beef, pork, or tofu, thinly sliced
- 2 tablespoons vegetable oil
- 3 tablespoons red curry paste
- 2 kaffir lime leaves, finely sliced (optional)
- 1 red bell pepper, thinly sliced
- 3-4 Thai bird's eye chilies, thinly sliced (adjust for spice preference)
- 2 tablespoons fish sauce (or soy sauce for a vegetarian version)
- 1 tablespoon oyster sauce (optional for non-vegetarian version)
- 1 tablespoon brown sugar
- 1/2 cup Thai basil leaves for garnish
- Cooked jasmine rice, for serving

Instructions:

Prepare Green Beans:
- Trim the ends of the green beans and cut them into bite-sized pieces.

Stir-Fry Green Beans:
- Heat vegetable oil in a wok or large skillet over medium-high heat. Add the green beans and stir-fry for 2-3 minutes until they are slightly tender but still crisp. Remove the green beans from the wok and set aside.

Stir-Fry Protein:
- In the same wok, add a bit more oil if needed. Stir-fry the thinly sliced chicken, beef, pork, or tofu until cooked through.

Add Red Curry Paste:
- Push the protein to one side of the wok. Add red curry paste to the empty side and stir for about 1-2 minutes until fragrant.

Combine Ingredients:
- Mix the red curry paste with the protein. Add sliced kaffir lime leaves (if using), thinly sliced red bell pepper, and Thai bird's eye chilies. Stir-fry for another 2-3 minutes.

Season the Stir-Fry:
- Pour in fish sauce (or soy sauce for a vegetarian version), oyster sauce (if using), and brown sugar. Stir well to combine.

Add Green Beans:

- Add the stir-fried green beans back to the wok. Toss everything together until the green beans are coated in the flavorful sauce.

Finish and Garnish:
- Add Thai basil leaves to the wok and stir-fry for an additional minute until the basil is wilted and aromatic.

Serve:
- Serve Pad Prik Khing hot over cooked jasmine rice.

Enjoy the vibrant and savory flavors of Stir-Fried Green Beans with Red Curry Paste! Adjust the spice level and ingredients according to your taste preferences.

Thai Basil Fried Rice

Ingredients:

- 3 cups cooked jasmine rice (preferably chilled)
- 1 lb (about 450g) chicken, beef, shrimp, or tofu, diced
- 2 tablespoons vegetable oil
- 4 cloves garlic, minced
- 2 Thai bird's eye chilies, finely chopped (adjust for spice preference)
- 1 bell pepper, diced
- 1 onion, thinly sliced
- 1 cup fresh basil leaves (Thai basil if available)
- 2 tablespoons soy sauce
- 1 tablespoon oyster sauce (optional)
- 1 tablespoon fish sauce
- 1 teaspoon sugar
- Fried or sunny-side-up eggs for serving (optional)
- Lime wedges for serving

Instructions:

Prepare Ingredients:
- Cook jasmine rice and set it aside to cool. Dice the protein (chicken, beef, shrimp, or tofu) into small pieces. Mince garlic, chop Thai bird's eye chilies, dice bell pepper, and thinly slice the onion. Pick basil leaves from the stems.

Stir-Fry Protein:
- Heat vegetable oil in a wok or large skillet over medium-high heat. Add minced garlic and chopped Thai bird's eye chilies. Stir-fry for about 30 seconds until fragrant. Add the diced protein and cook until browned and cooked through.

Add Vegetables:
- Add diced bell pepper and sliced onion to the wok. Stir-fry for an additional 2-3 minutes until the vegetables are tender-crisp.

Stir-Fry Rice:
- Add the chilled cooked jasmine rice to the wok. Break up any clumps and stir-fry the rice with the protein and vegetables.

Season with Sauces:

- Pour soy sauce, oyster sauce (if using), fish sauce, and sugar over the rice. Toss everything together until well combined.

Add Basil Leaves:
- Add fresh basil leaves to the wok. Toss until the basil wilts and imparts its aroma to the rice.

Adjust Seasoning:
- Taste and adjust the seasoning if needed. You can add more soy sauce, fish sauce, or sugar according to your taste.

Serve:
- Serve Thai Basil Fried Rice hot, optionally topped with a fried or sunny-side-up egg. Garnish with lime wedges on the side.

Enjoy the delicious and aromatic Thai Basil Fried Rice! Customize the protein and spice level based on your preferences.

Thai Cucumber Salad

Ingredients:

- 2 English cucumbers, thinly sliced
- 1/2 red onion, thinly sliced
- 1/4 cup chopped peanuts (optional, for garnish)

For the Dressing:

- 1/4 cup rice vinegar
- 2 tablespoons fish sauce (or soy sauce for a vegetarian version)
- 2 tablespoons sugar
- 1-2 Thai bird's eye chilies, finely chopped (adjust for spice preference)
- 1 clove garlic, minced
- 1 teaspoon sesame oil (optional)
- Fresh cilantro leaves for garnish

Instructions:

Prepare Cucumbers and Onion:
- Thinly slice the English cucumbers and red onion. You can use a mandoline for even slices.

Make the Dressing:
- In a bowl, whisk together rice vinegar, fish sauce (or soy sauce), sugar, chopped Thai bird's eye chilies, minced garlic, and sesame oil (if using). Stir until the sugar is dissolved.

Combine Ingredients:
- In a large bowl, combine the sliced cucumbers and red onion.

Add Dressing:
- Pour the dressing over the cucumber and onion mixture. Toss everything together until the vegetables are well coated with the dressing.

Chill:
- Cover the bowl and let the Thai Cucumber Salad chill in the refrigerator for at least 30 minutes to allow the flavors to meld.

Garnish:
- Before serving, garnish with chopped peanuts (if using) and fresh cilantro leaves.

Serve:
- Serve Thai Cucumber Salad as a refreshing side dish.

Enjoy the crisp and tangy flavors of Thai Cucumber Salad! Adjust the spice level and ingredients according to your taste preferences.

Thai Grilled Chicken (Gai Yang)

Ingredients:

For the Marinade:

- 1.5 lbs (about 700g) chicken thighs or drumsticks
- 4 cloves garlic, minced
- 2 tablespoons cilantro roots or stems, finely chopped
- 1 tablespoon soy sauce
- 1 tablespoon fish sauce
- 1 tablespoon oyster sauce (optional)
- 1 tablespoon sugar
- 1 teaspoon turmeric powder
- 1 teaspoon ground white pepper
- 2 tablespoons vegetable oil

For the Dipping Sauce:

- 3 tablespoons soy sauce
- 2 tablespoons fish sauce
- 2 tablespoons lime juice
- 1 tablespoon sugar
- 1-2 Thai bird's eye chilies, finely chopped (adjust for spice preference)

Instructions:

Prepare Chicken:
- If using chicken thighs, make a few shallow cuts on each piece to help the marinade penetrate. Place the chicken in a large bowl.

Make Marinade:
- In a separate bowl, mix together minced garlic, chopped cilantro roots or stems, soy sauce, fish sauce, oyster sauce (if using), sugar, turmeric powder, ground white pepper, and vegetable oil. This forms the marinade.

Marinate Chicken:
- Rub the marinade evenly over the chicken, ensuring it's well-coated. Allow the chicken to marinate for at least 1-2 hours or, ideally, overnight in the refrigerator for maximum flavor.

Grill Chicken:

- Preheat your grill or grill pan over medium-high heat. Grill the chicken for about 6-8 minutes per side or until fully cooked, with an internal temperature of 165°F (74°C).

Make Dipping Sauce:
- While the chicken is grilling, prepare the dipping sauce. In a bowl, whisk together soy sauce, fish sauce, lime juice, sugar, and chopped Thai bird's eye chilies.

Rest and Serve:
- Once the chicken is grilled, let it rest for a few minutes. Serve Thai Grilled Chicken with the prepared dipping sauce.

Garnish (Optional):
- Garnish the grilled chicken with additional chopped cilantro and lime wedges if desired.

Enjoy the delicious and aromatic flavors of Thai Grilled Chicken! Serve it with sticky rice or your favorite side dishes. Adjust the spice level and ingredients according to your taste preferences.

Pad Pak (Stir-Fried Vegetables)

Ingredients:

- 2 cups mixed vegetables (broccoli florets, bell peppers, carrots, baby corn, snow peas, etc.), sliced or chopped
- 2 tablespoons vegetable oil
- 2 cloves garlic, minced
- 1 tablespoon oyster sauce (for a vegetarian version, you can use soy sauce or a vegetarian stir-fry sauce)
- 1 tablespoon soy sauce
- 1 teaspoon sugar
- 1/4 cup water
- Optional: Thai bird's eye chilies, chopped (for spice)

Instructions:

Prepare Vegetables:
- Wash and chop the vegetables into bite-sized pieces.

Make Stir-Fry Sauce:
- In a small bowl, mix together oyster sauce (or soy sauce for a vegetarian version), soy sauce, sugar, and water. Set aside.

Stir-Fry Vegetables:
- Heat vegetable oil in a wok or large skillet over medium-high heat. Add minced garlic and Thai bird's eye chilies (if using) and stir for about 30 seconds until fragrant.

Add Vegetables:
- Add the mixed vegetables to the wok. Stir-fry for 3-4 minutes until they are slightly tender but still crisp.

Add Stir-Fry Sauce:
- Pour the prepared stir-fry sauce over the vegetables. Toss everything together to coat the vegetables evenly.

Cook Until Done:
- Continue stir-frying for an additional 2-3 minutes until the vegetables are cooked to your desired level of doneness. Be careful not to overcook; you want them to remain vibrant and slightly crisp.

Adjust Seasoning:
- Taste the stir-fried vegetables and adjust the seasoning if needed. You can add more soy sauce, sugar, or water to achieve the desired flavor.

Serve:
- Transfer the Pad Pak to a serving dish. Serve hot as a side dish or over steamed jasmine rice.

Enjoy this simple and versatile Stir-Fried Vegetables dish as a healthy addition to your Thai-inspired meals. Feel free to customize the vegetables based on your preferences.

Coconut Mango Pudding

Ingredients:

- 2 ripe mangoes, peeled and diced
- 1 can (14 oz) coconut milk
- 1/2 cup sugar (adjust according to your sweetness preference)
- 1/2 cup water
- 1/2 cup mango juice or puree
- 1/4 cup cornstarch
- 1/4 cup water (additional)
- 1 teaspoon vanilla extract (optional)
- Pinch of salt
- Fresh mint leaves for garnish (optional)

Instructions:

Prepare Mango Puree:
- In a blender, puree one of the ripe mangoes until smooth. Set aside.

Dice Mango:
- Dice the second ripe mango into small, bite-sized pieces. Set aside for later use as a topping.

Make Coconut Mango Base:
- In a saucepan, combine coconut milk, sugar, water, and mango juice or puree. Heat the mixture over medium heat, stirring to dissolve the sugar.

Prepare Cornstarch Slurry:
- In a small bowl, mix cornstarch with 1/4 cup of water to create a slurry.

Thicken the Mixture:
- Once the coconut mixture is warm, slowly whisk in the cornstarch slurry. Continue to cook, stirring constantly, until the mixture thickens. This should take about 5-7 minutes.

Add Mango Puree:
- Once the mixture has thickened, stir in the mango puree. Continue to cook for an additional 2-3 minutes.

Add Vanilla Extract and Salt (Optional):
- If desired, add vanilla extract and a pinch of salt for enhanced flavor. Stir to combine.

Cool and Set:

- Remove the saucepan from heat and let the Coconut Mango Pudding mixture cool slightly. Pour it into serving glasses or bowls.

Chill in the Refrigerator:
- Allow the Coconut Mango Pudding to cool to room temperature and then refrigerate for at least 2-3 hours, or until fully set.

Serve:
- Once set, top the Coconut Mango Pudding with diced mango pieces. Garnish with fresh mint leaves if desired.

Enjoy the luscious and tropical flavors of Coconut Mango Pudding! It's a perfect dessert to cool off on a warm day.

Spicy Thai Noodle Soup (Kuay Tiew Tom Yum)

Ingredients:

For the Soup:

- 8 oz (about 225g) rice noodles or egg noodles
- 4 cups chicken or vegetable broth
- 1 stalk lemongrass, bruised and cut into 2-inch pieces
- 3-4 kaffir lime leaves, torn into pieces
- 200g shrimp, peeled and deveined
- 200g chicken, thinly sliced (optional)
- 200g firm tofu, cubed (optional)
- 1 cup mushrooms, sliced
- 2 tomatoes, cut into wedges
- 2 tablespoons Tom Yum paste (available at Asian grocery stores)
- 2 tablespoons fish sauce (or soy sauce for a vegetarian version)
- 1-2 tablespoons lime juice
- 1 tablespoon sugar
- 1-2 Thai bird's eye chilies, sliced (adjust for spice preference)
- Fresh cilantro leaves for garnish
- Fresh Thai basil leaves for garnish (optional)

For Garnish:

- Bean sprouts
- Lime wedges
- Thai bird's eye chilies, sliced

Instructions:

Prepare Noodles:
- Cook rice noodles or egg noodles according to the package instructions. Drain and set aside.

Make Tom Yum Broth:

- In a pot, bring chicken or vegetable broth to a simmer. Add lemongrass and torn kaffir lime leaves to the broth. Let it simmer for about 5-7 minutes to infuse the flavors.

Add Proteins and Vegetables:
- Add shrimp, chicken (if using), tofu (if using), mushrooms, and tomatoes to the pot. Cook until the shrimp turns pink, and the chicken is cooked through.

Add Tom Yum Paste:
- Stir in Tom Yum paste and fish sauce (or soy sauce for a vegetarian version). Adjust the seasoning according to your taste.

Season the Soup:
- Add lime juice, sugar, and sliced Thai bird's eye chilies. Adjust the flavors to achieve the desired balance of sour, salty, and sweet.

Assemble Soup:
- Divide the cooked noodles among serving bowls. Ladle the hot Tom Yum soup over the noodles.

Garnish:
- Garnish the Spicy Thai Noodle Soup with bean sprouts, fresh cilantro leaves, Thai basil leaves (if using), and additional sliced Thai bird's eye chilies if you like it extra spicy.

Serve:
- Serve the Spicy Thai Noodle Soup hot with lime wedges on the side.

Enjoy the bold and spicy flavors of Kuay Tiew Tom Yum! Adjust the spice level and ingredients according to your taste preferences.

Thai Shrimp and Glass Noodle Salad)

Ingredients:

For the Salad:

- 8 oz (about 225g) glass noodles (bean thread noodles)
- 1 lb (about 450g) large shrimp, peeled and deveined
- 1 cup cherry tomatoes, halved
- 1 cucumber, thinly sliced
- 1 red onion, thinly sliced
- 1/2 cup fresh cilantro leaves
- 1/4 cup fresh mint leaves
- 1/4 cup roasted peanuts, chopped
- 1-2 Thai bird's eye chilies, thinly sliced (adjust for spice preference)

For the Dressing:

- 3 tablespoons fish sauce
- 3 tablespoons lime juice
- 2 tablespoons sugar
- 2 cloves garlic, minced
- 1-2 Thai bird's eye chilies, minced (adjust for spice preference)

Instructions:

Prepare Glass Noodles:
- Cook glass noodles according to the package instructions. Drain and set aside.

Blanch Shrimp:
- Bring a pot of water to a boil. Add the shrimp and cook for 2-3 minutes or until they turn pink and opaque. Remove the shrimp and place them in a bowl of ice water to cool.

Prepare Vegetables:
- In a large bowl, combine cherry tomatoes, sliced cucumber, thinly sliced red onion, fresh cilantro leaves, and fresh mint leaves.

Slice Shrimp:

- Once the shrimp are cool, slice them in half lengthwise.

Make Dressing:
- In a small bowl, whisk together fish sauce, lime juice, sugar, minced garlic, and minced Thai bird's eye chilies for the dressing.

Assemble Salad:
- Add the cooked glass noodles and sliced shrimp to the bowl of vegetables. Toss everything together gently.

Pour Dressing:
- Pour the prepared dressing over the salad. Toss again to ensure all the ingredients are well coated with the dressing.

Garnish:
- Garnish the Thai Shrimp and Glass Noodle Salad with chopped roasted peanuts and additional sliced Thai bird's eye chilies if you like it spicy.

Serve:
- Serve the salad immediately, either at room temperature or chilled.

Enjoy the vibrant and refreshing flavors of Yum Woon Sen, a perfect balance of textures and tastes. Adjust the spice level and ingredients according to your taste preferences.

Thai Chicken Lettuce Wraps

Ingredients:

For the Chicken Filling:

- 1 lb (about 450g) ground chicken
- 2 tablespoons vegetable oil
- 3 cloves garlic, minced
- 1 tablespoon fresh ginger, minced
- 1 red bell pepper, finely chopped
- 1 carrot, grated
- 1/2 cup water chestnuts, chopped
- 2 green onions, finely chopped
- 1/4 cup fresh cilantro, chopped
- 1/4 cup fresh mint leaves, chopped
- 1/4 cup hoisin sauce
- 2 tablespoons soy sauce
- 1 tablespoon fish sauce
- 1 tablespoon lime juice
- 1 teaspoon Sriracha sauce (adjust for spice preference)

For Serving:

- Iceberg or butter lettuce leaves, washed and separated
- Lime wedges
- Additional fresh cilantro and mint for garnish
- Crushed peanuts (optional)

Instructions:

Cook Chicken Filling:
- In a large skillet or wok, heat vegetable oil over medium-high heat. Add minced garlic and ginger, and sauté for about 1 minute until fragrant.

Brown Ground Chicken:
- Add ground chicken to the skillet and cook until browned, breaking it up with a spatula as it cooks.

Add Vegetables:

- Stir in chopped red bell pepper, grated carrot, and water chestnuts. Cook for an additional 2-3 minutes until the vegetables are tender.

Prepare Sauce:
- In a small bowl, mix together hoisin sauce, soy sauce, fish sauce, lime juice, and Sriracha sauce. Pour the sauce over the chicken mixture and stir to combine.

Finish with Herbs:
- Add chopped green onions, cilantro, and mint to the skillet. Stir well to incorporate the herbs into the chicken filling. Cook for an additional 1-2 minutes.

Adjust Seasoning:
- Taste the filling and adjust the seasoning if needed. You can add more soy sauce, fish sauce, or Sriracha according to your taste.

Assemble Lettuce Wraps:
- Spoon the Thai chicken filling into individual lettuce leaves.

Garnish and Serve:
- Garnish the wraps with additional fresh cilantro, mint, and crushed peanuts if desired. Serve the lettuce wraps with lime wedges on the side.

Enjoy assembling and devouring these delicious Thai Chicken Lettuce Wraps! They offer a wonderful combination of savory, sweet, and spicy flavors. Adjust the spice level and ingredients according to your preferences.

Thai Red Curry Noodles

Ingredients:

- 8 oz (about 225g) rice noodles or egg noodles
- 1 tablespoon vegetable oil
- 1 onion, thinly sliced
- 1 red bell pepper, thinly sliced
- 1 carrot, julienned
- 1 zucchini, julienned
- 2 tablespoons Thai red curry paste
- 1 can (14 oz) coconut milk
- 1 cup vegetable broth
- 1 tablespoon soy sauce
- 1 tablespoon brown sugar
- 1 lime, juiced
- 200g tofu, cubed (optional)
- Fresh cilantro leaves for garnish
- Crushed peanuts for garnish (optional)

Instructions:

Prepare Noodles:
- Cook rice noodles or egg noodles according to the package instructions. Drain and set aside.

Sauté Vegetables:
- Heat vegetable oil in a large wok or skillet over medium-high heat. Add sliced onion, red bell pepper, julienned carrot, and julienned zucchini. Stir-fry for 3-4 minutes until the vegetables are slightly tender but still crisp.

Add Red Curry Paste:
- Push the vegetables to one side of the wok. Add Thai red curry paste to the empty side and stir for about 1-2 minutes until fragrant.

Combine Ingredients:
- Mix the red curry paste with the sautéed vegetables. If using tofu, add the cubed tofu to the wok.

Add Coconut Milk and Broth:

- Pour in coconut milk and vegetable broth. Stir well to combine all the ingredients.

Season the Curry:
- Add soy sauce, brown sugar, and lime juice to the curry. Stir and let the mixture simmer for 5-7 minutes to allow the flavors to meld.

Adjust Seasoning:
- Taste the curry and adjust the seasoning if needed. You can add more soy sauce, brown sugar, or lime juice according to your taste.

Add Noodles:
- Add the cooked noodles to the wok. Toss everything together until the noodles are well coated in the red curry sauce.

Serve:
- Serve Thai Red Curry Noodles hot, garnished with fresh cilantro leaves and crushed peanuts if desired.

Enjoy the flavorful and comforting Thai Red Curry Noodles! Customize the spice level and ingredients according to your preferences.

Fried Tofu with Peanut Sauce

Ingredients:

For Fried Tofu:

- 1 block (about 14 oz) firm tofu, pressed and cut into cubes
- 1/2 cup cornstarch
- Vegetable oil for frying

For Peanut Sauce:

- 1/2 cup creamy peanut butter
- 3 tablespoons soy sauce
- 2 tablespoons rice vinegar
- 1 tablespoon sesame oil
- 1 tablespoon maple syrup or honey
- 1 clove garlic, minced
- 1 teaspoon grated fresh ginger
- 1/2 cup water (adjust for desired consistency)
- Red pepper flakes or Sriracha sauce to taste (optional)

For Garnish:

- Chopped green onions
- Sesame seeds
- Crushed peanuts
- Fresh cilantro leaves

Instructions:

Fry Tofu:
- Coat tofu cubes in cornstarch, shaking off excess. Heat vegetable oil in a pan over medium-high heat. Fry tofu until golden brown and crispy on all sides. Place fried tofu on a paper towel to absorb excess oil.

Make Peanut Sauce:
- In a bowl, whisk together peanut butter, soy sauce, rice vinegar, sesame oil, maple syrup or honey, minced garlic, grated ginger, and water. Adjust the consistency with more water if needed. Add red pepper flakes or Sriracha for heat if desired.

Coat Tofu with Peanut Sauce:
- Toss the fried tofu in the prepared peanut sauce until well coated.

Garnish and Serve:
- Garnish the Fried Tofu with Peanut Sauce with chopped green onions, sesame seeds, crushed peanuts, and fresh cilantro leaves.

Serve:
- Serve the dish as an appetizer, snack, or as part of a meal. Enjoy it with rice or noodles.

This Fried Tofu with Peanut Sauce is a delightful combination of textures and flavors. Adjust the peanut sauce to your taste preferences, and feel free to experiment with additional toppings.

Thai Sweet Chili Sauce

Ingredients:

- 1 cup granulated sugar
- 1/2 cup water
- 1/2 cup rice vinegar
- 2 cloves garlic, minced
- 1-2 red chili peppers, finely chopped (adjust for spice preference)
- 1 tablespoon cornstarch
- 2 tablespoons water (for cornstarch slurry)
- 1/2 teaspoon salt

Instructions:

Prepare Chili Peppers and Garlic:
- Finely chop the red chili peppers and mince the garlic.

Make Cornstarch Slurry:
- In a small bowl, mix cornstarch with 2 tablespoons of water to create a slurry. Set aside.

Combine Ingredients:
- In a saucepan, combine granulated sugar, water, rice vinegar, minced garlic, chopped red chili peppers, and salt. Stir well to dissolve the sugar.

Boil and Simmer:
- Bring the mixture to a boil over medium-high heat. Once boiling, reduce the heat to low and let it simmer for about 5-7 minutes, allowing the flavors to meld.

Thicken with Cornstarch Slurry:
- Stir the cornstarch slurry to ensure it's well mixed, and then add it to the saucepan. Stir continuously until the sauce thickens, which should take about 1-2 minutes.

Cool and Store:
- Remove the saucepan from heat and let the Thai Sweet Chili Sauce cool to room temperature.

Strain (Optional):
- If you prefer a smoother sauce, you can strain the sauce through a fine mesh sieve to remove the chili pepper and garlic bits.

Store:

- Transfer the sweet chili sauce to a clean, airtight container or glass jar. Store it in the refrigerator.

Serve:
- Thai Sweet Chili Sauce is ready to be used as a dipping sauce, glaze, or condiment.

Enjoy your homemade Thai Sweet Chili Sauce with spring rolls, grilled chicken, seafood, or any dish that could use a touch of sweet and spicy goodness! Adjust the quantity of chili peppers based on your spice preference.

Thai Pineapple Fried Quinoa

Ingredients:

- 1 cup quinoa, rinsed and cooked according to package instructions
- 1 tablespoon vegetable oil
- 1 small onion, finely chopped
- 2 cloves garlic, minced
- 1 cup diced pineapple (fresh or canned)
- 1 red bell pepper, diced
- 1 carrot, diced
- 1/2 cup frozen peas
- 2 green onions, chopped
- 2 eggs, beaten (optional)
- 3 tablespoons soy sauce
- 1 tablespoon fish sauce (optional for added umami)
- 1 tablespoon curry powder
- 1/2 teaspoon turmeric powder
- Salt and pepper to taste
- Fresh cilantro leaves for garnish
- Lime wedges for serving

Instructions:

Cook Quinoa:
- Rinse the quinoa under cold water and cook it according to the package instructions. Once cooked, set aside.

Prepare Vegetables:
- Heat vegetable oil in a large skillet or wok over medium-high heat. Add chopped onion and garlic, sauté until fragrant and slightly golden.

Add Vegetables:
- Add diced pineapple, red bell pepper, carrot, and frozen peas to the skillet. Stir-fry for 3-4 minutes until the vegetables are tender but still crisp.

Push Vegetables to One Side:
- Push the vegetables to one side of the skillet to create space for the eggs (if using).

Scramble Eggs (Optional):
- Pour beaten eggs into the empty side of the skillet. Scramble them until cooked, and then mix them with the vegetables.

Combine Quinoa:
- Add the cooked quinoa to the skillet. Toss everything together until well combined.

Season with Sauces and Spices:
- Drizzle soy sauce, fish sauce (if using), curry powder, and turmeric powder over the quinoa mixture. Stir to evenly distribute the flavors.

Adjust Seasoning:
- Taste the Thai Pineapple Fried Quinoa and adjust the seasoning with salt and pepper as needed.

Finish with Green Onions:
- Add chopped green onions and toss to combine.

Serve:
- Garnish with fresh cilantro leaves and serve the Thai Pineapple Fried Quinoa hot. Serve with lime wedges on the side.

Enjoy this flavorful and nutritious Thai Pineapple Fried Quinoa as a main dish or a side. Feel free to customize the recipe by adding your favorite protein, such as tofu, shrimp, or chicken.

Thai Basil Pork (Pad Kra Pao Moo)

Ingredients:

- 1 lb (about 450g) ground pork
- 2 tablespoons vegetable oil
- 4 cloves garlic, minced
- 4 Thai bird's eye chilies, finely chopped (adjust for spice preference)
- 1 cup fresh Thai basil leaves (holy basil or sweet basil can be used)
- 2 tablespoons oyster sauce
- 1 tablespoon soy sauce
- 1 teaspoon fish sauce
- 1 teaspoon sugar
- 1/4 cup chicken broth or water
- Fried egg (optional, for serving)
- Jasmine rice, for serving

Instructions:

Prepare Ingredients:
- Ensure that the ground pork, garlic, Thai bird's eye chilies, and Thai basil are ready to use.

Stir-Fry Ground Pork:
- Heat vegetable oil in a wok or large skillet over medium-high heat. Add minced garlic and chopped Thai bird's eye chilies. Stir-fry for about 30 seconds until fragrant.

Add Ground Pork:
- Add the ground pork to the wok. Break it apart with a spatula and cook until browned.

Make Sauce:
- In a small bowl, mix together oyster sauce, soy sauce, fish sauce, and sugar to create the sauce.

Combine Ingredients:
- Once the pork is browned, add the prepared sauce to the wok. Stir to coat the pork evenly.

Add Basil Leaves:
- Add fresh Thai basil leaves to the wok. Toss everything together until the basil wilts and is evenly distributed.

Adjust Seasoning:

- Taste the Thai Basil Pork and adjust the seasoning if needed. You can add more soy sauce, fish sauce, or sugar according to your taste.

Add Broth or Water:
- Pour chicken broth or water into the wok to create a bit of sauce. Stir well.

Serve:
- Serve Thai Basil Pork over jasmine rice. Optionally, top it with a fried egg.

Enjoy the bold and aromatic flavors of Pad Kra Pao Moo! Adjust the spice level and ingredients according to your taste preferences.

Thai Chili Garlic Prawns

Ingredients:

- 1 lb (about 450g) large prawns, peeled and deveined
- 2 tablespoons vegetable oil
- 4 cloves garlic, minced
- 2 Thai bird's eye chilies, finely chopped (adjust for spice preference)
- 2 tablespoons oyster sauce
- 1 tablespoon fish sauce
- 1 tablespoon soy sauce
- 1 tablespoon sugar
- 1 tablespoon water
- 1/2 cup fresh cilantro leaves, chopped (for garnish)
- Lime wedges, for serving

Instructions:

Prepare Prawns:
- Ensure that the prawns are peeled, deveined, and patted dry with paper towels.

Heat Oil:
- Heat vegetable oil in a wok or large skillet over medium-high heat.

Sauté Garlic and Chilies:
- Add minced garlic and chopped Thai bird's eye chilies to the hot oil. Stir-fry for about 30 seconds until fragrant.

Add Prawns:
- Add the prawns to the wok. Cook for 2-3 minutes, stirring occasionally, until they start to turn pink.

Make Sauce:
- In a small bowl, mix together oyster sauce, fish sauce, soy sauce, sugar, and water to create the sauce.

Add Sauce to Prawns:
- Pour the sauce over the prawns in the wok. Toss the prawns to coat them evenly in the sauce.

Cook Until Done:
- Continue to cook the prawns for an additional 2-3 minutes until they are fully cooked and have absorbed the flavors of the sauce.

Adjust Seasoning:

- Taste the Thai Chili Garlic Prawns and adjust the seasoning if needed. You can add more soy sauce, fish sauce, or sugar according to your taste.

Garnish:
- Garnish the dish with chopped fresh cilantro leaves.

Serve:
- Serve Thai Chili Garlic Prawns hot, with lime wedges on the side.

Enjoy the spicy and savory goodness of Thai Chili Garlic Prawns! Serve them over steamed jasmine rice or noodles for a complete and satisfying meal. Adjust the spice level according to your preference.

Thai Corn Fritters

Ingredients:

- 2 cups corn kernels (fresh or frozen)
- 1/2 cup all-purpose flour
- 1/4 cup rice flour
- 1/2 teaspoon baking powder
- 1/2 teaspoon turmeric powder
- 1/2 teaspoon cayenne pepper (adjust for spice preference)
- 1/2 teaspoon sugar
- 1/2 teaspoon salt
- 1/4 cup coconut milk
- 1 egg, beaten
- 2 kaffir lime leaves, finely chopped (optional)
- 2 tablespoons red curry paste (optional, for added flavor)
- Vegetable oil for frying
- Sweet chili sauce, for dipping

Instructions:

Prepare Corn Mixture:
- If using fresh corn, remove the kernels from the cob. If using frozen corn, thaw and pat dry with paper towels. Place the corn in a large mixing bowl.

Make Batter:
- In a separate bowl, whisk together all-purpose flour, rice flour, baking powder, turmeric powder, cayenne pepper, sugar, and salt.

Combine Ingredients:
- Add the dry ingredients to the corn in the mixing bowl. Mix well.

Add Wet Ingredients:
- Add coconut milk, beaten egg, chopped kaffir lime leaves (if using), and red curry paste (if using) to the corn mixture. Stir until all ingredients are well combined.

Heat Oil:
- Heat vegetable oil in a deep pan or wok over medium-high heat.

Fry Corn Fritters:

- Once the oil is hot, drop spoonfuls of the corn mixture into the oil, frying a few fritters at a time. Fry until they are golden brown and crispy, about 2-3 minutes per side.

Drain and Repeat:
- Remove the corn fritters from the oil using a slotted spoon and place them on a plate lined with paper towels to drain any excess oil. Repeat the process until all the batter is used.

Serve:
- Serve the Thai Corn Fritters hot, with sweet chili sauce for dipping.

Enjoy these crispy and flavorful Thai Corn Fritters as a tasty snack or appetizer. The combination of sweet corn, aromatic spices, and the crispy texture makes them a crowd-pleaser. Adjust the spice level according to your taste preferences.

Tom Yum Fried Rice

Ingredients:

- 2 cups cooked jasmine rice (preferably chilled or leftover rice)
- 200g shrimp, peeled and deveined
- 1 chicken breast, thinly sliced
- 2 eggs, beaten
- 1 cup mixed vegetables (bell peppers, peas, carrots), diced
- 3 tablespoons Tom Yum paste
- 2 tablespoons fish sauce
- 1 tablespoon soy sauce
- 1 tablespoon vegetable oil
- 1 tablespoon garlic, minced
- 1 tablespoon ginger, grated
- 2 green onions, chopped
- Fresh cilantro leaves for garnish
- Lime wedges for serving

Instructions:

Prepare Ingredients:
- Ensure that the cooked jasmine rice is chilled or leftover. Peel and devein the shrimp, thinly slice the chicken breast, beat the eggs, and dice the mixed vegetables.

Heat Wok or Skillet:
- Heat vegetable oil in a wok or large skillet over medium-high heat.

Stir-Fry Shrimp and Chicken:
- Add the shrimp and sliced chicken to the wok. Stir-fry until the shrimp turn pink and the chicken is cooked through.

Add Garlic and Ginger:
- Add minced garlic and grated ginger to the wok. Stir-fry for about 1-2 minutes until fragrant.

Add Mixed Vegetables:
- Add the diced mixed vegetables to the wok. Stir-fry for an additional 2-3 minutes until the vegetables are tender-crisp.

Push Ingredients to One Side:
- Push the ingredients to one side of the wok, creating space for the eggs.

Scramble Eggs:

- Pour the beaten eggs into the empty side of the wok. Allow them to set slightly before scrambling them. Mix the eggs with the other ingredients.

Add Tom Yum Paste:
- Add Tom Yum paste to the wok. Stir to coat the ingredients evenly.

Season with Sauces:
- Pour fish sauce and soy sauce over the fried rice. Stir well to combine.

Add Chilled Rice:
- Add the chilled or leftover jasmine rice to the wok. Stir-fry, breaking up any clumps, until the rice is well coated with the flavors.

Finish with Green Onions:
- Add chopped green onions to the fried rice. Stir to incorporate.

Adjust Seasoning:
- Taste the Tom Yum Fried Rice and adjust the seasoning if needed. You can add more Tom Yum paste, fish sauce, or soy sauce according to your taste.

Serve:
- Garnish the Tom Yum Fried Rice with fresh cilantro leaves and serve hot. Serve with lime wedges on the side for squeezing over the rice.

Enjoy the bold and zesty flavors of Tom Yum Fried Rice! It's a delicious and aromatic dish that combines the essence of Tom Yum soup with the comfort of fried rice. Adjust the spice level according to your preference.

Thai Style Grilled Fish

Ingredients:

- 1 whole fish (such as tilapia, sea bass, or snapper), cleaned and scaled
- 4-5 stalks lemongrass, bruised
- 4-5 kaffir lime leaves
- 3-4 cloves garlic, minced
- 2 tablespoons fresh cilantro, chopped
- 2 tablespoons fish sauce
- 1 tablespoon soy sauce
- 1 tablespoon oyster sauce
- 1 tablespoon sugar
- 1 teaspoon black pepper
- 2 tablespoons vegetable oil
- Fresh cilantro and lime wedges for garnish

Instructions:

Prepare the Fish:
- Ensure that the fish is cleaned, scaled, and gutted. Make diagonal cuts on both sides of the fish, allowing the marinade to penetrate.

Make the Marinade:
- In a bowl, mix together minced garlic, chopped cilantro, fish sauce, soy sauce, oyster sauce, sugar, black pepper, and vegetable oil.

Marinate the Fish:
- Rub the marinade all over the fish, including inside the cuts and the cavity. Allow the fish to marinate for at least 30 minutes to allow the flavors to infuse.

Prepare the Grill:
- Preheat a grill to medium-high heat. If using charcoal, wait until the coals are hot.

Assemble the Grill Pack:
- Lay out a large piece of aluminum foil. Place half of the lemongrass stalks on the foil, forming a bed for the fish. Lay the fish on top of the lemongrass.

Add Aromatics:
- Stuff the fish cavity with the remaining lemongrass stalks and kaffir lime leaves.

Grill the Fish:
- Place the foil-wrapped fish on the preheated grill. Close the lid and grill for about 15-20 minutes, depending on the size of the fish. Turn the fish halfway through the cooking time.

Check for Doneness:
- The fish is done when the flesh is opaque and easily flakes with a fork. The skin should be crispy from the grilling process.

Garnish and Serve:
- Carefully transfer the grilled fish to a serving platter. Garnish with fresh cilantro and serve with lime wedges on the side.

Enjoy the authentic flavors of Thai Style Grilled Fish! Serve it with steamed jasmine rice and your favorite Thai dipping sauces for a complete and delicious meal.

Thai Coconut Pancakes (Kanom Krok)

Ingredients:

For the Batter:

- 1 cup rice flour
- 1 cup coconut milk
- 1 cup water
- 1/2 cup sugar
- 1/4 teaspoon salt

For the Filling:

- 1 cup shredded coconut (fresh or desiccated)
- 1/4 cup palm sugar or brown sugar
- 1/4 cup water

Instructions:

- Prepare the Batter:
  - In a mixing bowl, whisk together rice flour, coconut milk, water, sugar, and salt until you have a smooth batter. Let the batter rest for 30 minutes.
- Prepare the Filling:
  - In a saucepan, combine shredded coconut, palm sugar (or brown sugar), and water. Cook over medium heat until the sugar dissolves and the mixture becomes sticky. Set aside.
- Heat the Pan:
  - Preheat a Kanom Krok pan or a small-sized pancake pan over medium heat. If you don't have a specific pan, you can use a mini muffin tin.
- Grease the Pan:
  - Lightly grease the pancake cups with oil or coconut oil.
- Pour the Batter:
  - Pour a small amount of the batter into each cup, filling them about halfway.
- Add the Filling:
  - Add a small amount of the coconut and sugar filling into the center of each pancake.
- Cover and Cook:

- Cover the pan and cook for 3-5 minutes until the edges are crispy, and the center is set.

Flip and Cook:
- Carefully flip each pancake using a spoon or chopstick. Cook for an additional 2-3 minutes until the other side is golden brown.

Remove from Pan:
- Use a spoon or a skewer to gently remove the Kanom Krok from the pan.

Repeat:
- Repeat the process with the remaining batter and filling.

Serve:
- Serve Thai Coconut Pancakes warm, either as a snack or a sweet treat. Enjoy the crispy edges and the soft, coconut-infused center.

These Thai Coconut Pancakes are a delightful and authentic treat. You can experiment with the filling or even add toppings like corn or spring onions for a savory version. Adjust the sugar to your liking, as sweetness preferences vary.

Thai Green Curry Noodles

Ingredients:

For the Green Curry Paste:

- 2 green Thai bird's eye chilies (adjust for spice preference)
- 2 shallots, chopped
- 3 cloves garlic, minced
- 1 lemongrass stalk, thinly sliced
- 1 thumb-sized piece of galangal or ginger, chopped
- 1 kaffir lime zest (optional)
- 1 tablespoon coriander powder
- 1 teaspoon cumin powder
- 1/2 teaspoon white pepper
- 1/2 teaspoon shrimp paste (optional, for authenticity)
- 2 tablespoons cilantro stems, chopped
- 1 tablespoon vegetable oil

For the Noodles:

- 8 oz (about 225g) rice noodles or egg noodles
- 1 tablespoon vegetable oil
- 1 can (14 oz) coconut milk
- 1 cup chicken or vegetable broth
- 1 cup mixed vegetables (bell peppers, snap peas, carrots)
- 200g chicken, shrimp, or tofu, cooked (optional)
- 2 tablespoons fish sauce (or soy sauce for a vegetarian version)
- 1 tablespoon brown sugar
- Fresh cilantro and lime wedges for garnish

Instructions:

1. Prepare the Green Curry Paste:

   - In a blender or mortar and pestle, combine all the green curry paste ingredients. Blend or grind into a smooth paste.

2. Cook the Noodles:

- Cook the rice noodles or egg noodles according to the package instructions. Drain and set aside.

3. Make the Green Curry Sauce:

- Heat vegetable oil in a large pan or wok over medium-high heat. Add the green curry paste and sauté for 1-2 minutes until fragrant.
- Pour in the coconut milk and chicken or vegetable broth. Stir well to combine.

4. Add Vegetables and Protein:

- Add the mixed vegetables and cooked chicken, shrimp, or tofu to the curry sauce. Simmer for 5-7 minutes until the vegetables are tender and the protein is heated through.

5. Season the Curry:

- Stir in fish sauce (or soy sauce for a vegetarian version) and brown sugar. Taste and adjust the seasoning if needed.

6. Combine with Noodles:

- Add the cooked noodles to the curry mixture. Toss everything together until the noodles are well coated in the green curry sauce.

7. Serve:

- Serve Thai Green Curry Noodles hot, garnished with fresh cilantro leaves and lime wedges on the side.

Enjoy the aromatic and flavorful Thai Green Curry Noodles! Customize the spice level and ingredients according to your preferences.

Thai Eggplant Stir-Fry

Ingredients:

- 1 lb (about 450g) Thai eggplants, halved or quartered
- 1/2 cup firm tofu, cubed (optional)
- 1 red bell pepper, sliced
- 1 green bell pepper, sliced
- 1 onion, thinly sliced
- 3 cloves garlic, minced
- 1 thumb-sized piece of ginger, grated
- 2 tablespoons vegetable oil
- 2 tablespoons soy sauce
- 1 tablespoon oyster sauce (or vegetarian oyster sauce for a vegetarian version)
- 1 tablespoon fish sauce (or soy sauce for a vegetarian version)
- 1 tablespoon brown sugar
- 1 teaspoon chili paste or Sriracha (adjust for spice preference)
- Fresh basil leaves for garnish
- Cooked jasmine rice for serving

Instructions:

Prepare Vegetables:
- Cut the Thai eggplants into halves or quarters, depending on their size. Slice the red and green bell peppers, and thinly slice the onion.

Stir-Fry Tofu (Optional):
- Heat 1 tablespoon of vegetable oil in a wok or large skillet over medium-high heat. Add the cubed tofu and stir-fry until golden brown. Remove the tofu from the pan and set aside.

Sauté Aromatics:
- In the same wok, add another tablespoon of vegetable oil. Add minced garlic and grated ginger. Sauté for about 30 seconds until fragrant.

Add Vegetables:
- Add the sliced Thai eggplants, red bell pepper, green bell pepper, and onion to the wok. Stir-fry for 5-7 minutes until the vegetables are tender but still crisp.

Make Sauce:
- In a small bowl, whisk together soy sauce, oyster sauce, fish sauce, brown sugar, and chili paste (or Sriracha).

Combine Ingredients:
- If using tofu, return it to the wok. Pour the sauce over the vegetables and tofu. Toss everything together to coat evenly.

Cook Until Heated Through:
- Continue to stir-fry for an additional 2-3 minutes until the ingredients are heated through and well coated with the sauce.

Adjust Seasoning:
- Taste the stir-fry and adjust the seasoning if needed. You can add more soy sauce, fish sauce, or sugar according to your taste.

Garnish and Serve:
- Garnish the Thai Eggplant Stir-Fry with fresh basil leaves. Serve over jasmine rice.

Enjoy this flavorful and colorful Thai Eggplant Stir-Fry as a delicious and satisfying meal. Adjust the spice level and ingredients according to your preferences.

Thai Red Curry Chicken Satay

Ingredients:

For the Marinade:

- 1 lb (about 450g) chicken breast or thighs, cut into thin strips
- 1/4 cup Thai red curry paste
- 2 tablespoons coconut milk
- 1 tablespoon fish sauce
- 1 tablespoon soy sauce
- 1 tablespoon brown sugar
- 1 tablespoon vegetable oil
- Bamboo skewers, soaked in water for at least 30 minutes

For the Peanut Dipping Sauce:

- 1/2 cup creamy peanut butter
- 1/4 cup coconut milk
- 2 tablespoons soy sauce
- 1 tablespoon brown sugar
- 1 tablespoon lime juice
- 1 teaspoon Thai red curry paste (adjust for spice preference)
- Water to adjust consistency

For Garnish:

- Chopped cilantro
- Crushed peanuts
- Lime wedges

Instructions:

Prepare the Marinade:
- In a bowl, mix together red curry paste, coconut milk, fish sauce, soy sauce, brown sugar, and vegetable oil to create the marinade.

Marinate the Chicken:
- Place the chicken strips in the marinade, ensuring they are well coated. Cover and refrigerate for at least 2 hours or overnight for the flavors to meld.

Preheat the Grill:
- Preheat a grill or grill pan over medium-high heat.

Skewer the Chicken:
- Thread the marinated chicken strips onto the soaked bamboo skewers.

Grill the Satay:
- Grill the chicken satay for 3-4 minutes on each side or until fully cooked and slightly charred.

Prepare the Peanut Dipping Sauce:
- In a small saucepan over low heat, combine peanut butter, coconut milk, soy sauce, brown sugar, lime juice, and red curry paste. Stir until well combined and heated through. Adjust the consistency with water if needed.

Serve:
- Arrange the grilled Thai Red Curry Chicken Satay on a serving platter. Garnish with chopped cilantro and crushed peanuts.

Dip and Enjoy:
- Serve the chicken satay with the prepared peanut dipping sauce and lime wedges on the side.

Enjoy the delicious Thai Red Curry Chicken Satay as an appetizer or main dish. The combination of the flavorful marinade and the rich peanut sauce creates a tasty and satisfying dish. Adjust the spice level to your liking by modifying the amount of red curry paste.

Thai Glass Noodle Salad (Yum Woon Sen)

Ingredients:

For the Salad:

- 100g (about 3.5 oz) dried glass noodles
- 1 cup cooked and peeled shrimp, chopped into bite-sized pieces
- 1 cup ground chicken or pork, cooked and cooled
- 1 cup cherry tomatoes, halved
- 1 cup cucumber, thinly sliced
- 1/2 cup red onion, thinly sliced
- 1/4 cup cilantro leaves, chopped
- 1/4 cup mint leaves, torn
- 1/4 cup roasted peanuts, crushed

For the Dressing:

- 3 tablespoons fish sauce
- 2 tablespoons lime juice
- 1 tablespoon soy sauce
- 1 tablespoon sugar
- 1-2 Thai bird's eye chilies, finely chopped (adjust for spice preference)

Instructions:

Prepare Glass Noodles:
- Cook the glass noodles according to the package instructions. Once cooked, drain and rinse with cold water. Cut the noodles into shorter lengths with kitchen scissors.

Make the Dressing:
- In a small bowl, whisk together fish sauce, lime juice, soy sauce, sugar, and chopped Thai bird's eye chilies. Adjust the seasoning to your taste.

Assemble the Salad:
- In a large mixing bowl, combine the cooked glass noodles, chopped shrimp, ground chicken or pork, cherry tomatoes, cucumber, red onion, cilantro, and mint leaves.

Add Dressing:

- Pour the dressing over the salad ingredients. Toss everything together until well combined and evenly coated with the dressing.

Chill and Marinate:
- Cover the bowl and refrigerate the Thai Glass Noodle Salad for at least 30 minutes to allow the flavors to marinate.

Serve:
- Just before serving, sprinkle crushed roasted peanuts over the salad for added crunch.

Garnish and Enjoy:
- Garnish the Thai Glass Noodle Salad with additional cilantro and mint leaves. Serve chilled and enjoy!

This Thai Glass Noodle Salad is a light and refreshing dish with a perfect balance of flavors. Customize the salad with your favorite vegetables or protein choices. Adjust the level of spiciness by adding more or fewer Thai bird's eye chilies.

Thai Cashew Tofu Stir-Fry

Ingredients:

- 1 block (14 oz) firm tofu, pressed and cubed
- 1 cup unsalted cashews
- 1 red bell pepper, sliced
- 1 yellow bell pepper, sliced
- 1 cup broccoli florets
- 1 carrot, julienned
- 3 cloves garlic, minced
- 1 tablespoon vegetable oil
- 2 tablespoons soy sauce
- 1 tablespoon oyster sauce (or vegetarian oyster sauce for a vegetarian version)
- 1 tablespoon hoisin sauce
- 1 tablespoon fish sauce (or soy sauce for a vegetarian version)
- 1 tablespoon brown sugar
- 1 teaspoon chili paste or Sriracha (adjust for spice preference)
- Fresh cilantro leaves for garnish
- Cooked jasmine rice for serving

Instructions:

Press and Cube Tofu:
- Press the tofu to remove excess moisture. Cut it into bite-sized cubes.

Toast Cashews:
- In a dry wok or skillet, toast the cashews over medium heat until they are lightly browned and fragrant. Remove from the wok and set aside.

Sauté Tofu:
- Heat vegetable oil in the wok over medium-high heat. Add the tofu cubes and stir-fry until they are golden brown on all sides. Remove tofu from the wok and set aside.

Cook Vegetables:
- In the same wok, add a bit more oil if needed. Add minced garlic and sauté for about 30 seconds until fragrant. Add the sliced bell peppers, broccoli, and julienned carrot. Stir-fry for 3-4 minutes until the vegetables are crisp-tender.

Prepare Sauce:

- In a small bowl, mix together soy sauce, oyster sauce, hoisin sauce, fish sauce, brown sugar, and chili paste (or Sriracha).

Combine Ingredients:
- Add the cooked tofu and toasted cashews back to the wok. Pour the sauce over the ingredients. Toss everything together until well coated and heated through.

Adjust Seasoning:
- Taste the stir-fry and adjust the seasoning if needed. You can add more soy sauce, fish sauce, or sugar according to your taste.

Serve:
- Serve the Thai Cashew Tofu Stir-Fry over jasmine rice. Garnish with fresh cilantro leaves.

Enjoy this flavorful and nutritious Thai Cashew Tofu Stir-Fry as a satisfying and wholesome meal. Adjust the level of spiciness and customize the vegetables according to your preferences.

Thai Style BBQ Pork Skewers

Ingredients:

For the Marinade:

- 1 lb (about 450g) pork tenderloin or pork shoulder, thinly sliced
- 3 tablespoons oyster sauce
- 2 tablespoons soy sauce
- 2 tablespoons fish sauce
- 2 tablespoons honey or brown sugar
- 1 tablespoon garlic, minced
- 1 tablespoon cilantro roots or stems, finely chopped
- 1 teaspoon ground white pepper
- 1 teaspoon sesame oil

For the Dipping Sauce:

- 1/4 cup soy sauce
- 2 tablespoons rice vinegar
- 1 tablespoon honey or brown sugar
- 1 clove garlic, minced
- 1 Thai bird's eye chili, finely chopped (optional for heat)
- Chopped peanuts for garnish (optional)

For Skewers:

- Bamboo skewers, soaked in water for at least 30 minutes

Instructions:

Prepare the Marinade:
- In a bowl, combine oyster sauce, soy sauce, fish sauce, honey or brown sugar, minced garlic, chopped cilantro roots or stems, ground white pepper, and sesame oil. Mix well to create the marinade.

Marinate the Pork:
- Place the thinly sliced pork in the marinade, ensuring each piece is well coated. Cover and refrigerate for at least 2 hours, or ideally overnight, for the flavors to meld.

Skewer the Pork:

- Thread the marinated pork slices onto the soaked bamboo skewers. Leave a bit of space between each slice for even cooking.

Preheat the Grill:

- Preheat a grill or grill pan over medium-high heat.

Grill the Skewers:

- Grill the pork skewers for about 3-4 minutes on each side or until they are fully cooked and have a nice char.

Make the Dipping Sauce:

- In a small bowl, mix together soy sauce, rice vinegar, honey or brown sugar, minced garlic, and chopped Thai bird's eye chili (if using).

Serve:

- Serve the Thai Style BBQ Pork Skewers hot off the grill, with the dipping sauce on the side. Garnish with chopped peanuts if desired.

Enjoy these flavorful Thai BBQ Pork Skewers as a delicious appetizer or main course. The marinade imparts a sweet and savory taste to the pork, and the dipping sauce adds a tangy kick. Adjust the level of spiciness by modifying the amount of Thai bird's eye chili in the dipping sauce.

Coconut Banana Fritters

Ingredients:

- 3 ripe bananas, mashed
- 1 cup all-purpose flour
- 1/4 cup sugar
- 1/2 cup shredded coconut (sweetened or unsweetened)
- 1 teaspoon baking powder
- 1/4 teaspoon salt
- 1/2 cup coconut milk
- 1 teaspoon vanilla extract
- Vegetable oil for frying
- Powdered sugar for dusting (optional)

Instructions:

Prepare the Batter:
- In a large mixing bowl, combine mashed bananas, all-purpose flour, sugar, shredded coconut, baking powder, and salt.

Add Wet Ingredients:
- Add coconut milk and vanilla extract to the dry ingredients. Stir until well combined, creating a thick batter.

Heat Oil:
- Heat vegetable oil in a deep pan or skillet over medium heat. The oil should be hot enough for frying.

Drop Spoonfuls into Oil:
- Using a spoon, drop spoonfuls of the banana batter into the hot oil. Be careful not to overcrowd the pan.

Fry Until Golden Brown:
- Fry the fritters until they are golden brown on both sides, turning them to ensure even cooking. This usually takes about 2-3 minutes per side.

Drain Excess Oil:
- Remove the fritters from the oil using a slotted spoon and place them on a plate lined with paper towels to drain any excess oil.

Dust with Powdered Sugar (Optional):
- If desired, dust the Coconut Banana Fritters with powdered sugar for extra sweetness.

Serve Warm:

- Serve the Coconut Banana Fritters warm. They can be enjoyed on their own or with a scoop of vanilla ice cream for a decadent dessert.

These Coconut Banana Fritters are a delicious treat with a crispy exterior and a soft, sweet interior. The addition of coconut adds a delightful tropical twist. Feel free to customize the recipe by adding a pinch of cinnamon or nutmeg to enhance the flavor.

Thai Green Papaya Soup

Ingredients:

- 1 can (14 oz) coconut milk
- 2 cups chicken broth
- 1 lemongrass stalk, bruised and cut into 2-inch pieces
- 3-4 slices galangal or ginger
- 2-3 kaffir lime leaves, torn into pieces
- 200g chicken breast, sliced into thin strips
- 1 cup mushrooms, sliced
- 1 medium-sized tomato, cut into wedges
- 1 small onion, sliced
- 2 tablespoons fish sauce
- 1-2 tablespoons lime juice
- 1 teaspoon sugar
- Thai bird's eye chilies, sliced (optional for heat)
- Fresh cilantro leaves for garnish

Instructions:

Prepare Ingredients:
- Slice the chicken, mushrooms, tomato, and onion. Bruise the lemongrass, and tear the kaffir lime leaves.

Cook Aromatics:
- In a pot, combine coconut milk and chicken broth. Add lemongrass, galangal, and kaffir lime leaves. Bring to a gentle simmer over medium heat for about 5 minutes to infuse the flavors.

Add Chicken and Vegetables:
- Add sliced chicken, mushrooms, tomato, and onion to the pot. Simmer until the chicken is cooked through and vegetables are tender.

Season the Soup:
- Stir in fish sauce, lime juice, sugar, and Thai bird's eye chilies (if using). Adjust the seasoning to your taste.

Serve:
- Remove lemongrass, galangal slices, and kaffir lime leaves before serving. Ladle the soup into bowls.

Garnish:
- Garnish with fresh cilantro leaves.

Enjoy this Thai-inspired Tom Kha Gai soup with its rich coconut broth and aromatic herbs. Adjust the ingredients and spice level according to your preferences.

Thai Basil Chicken Meatballs

Ingredients:

For the Meatballs:

- 1 lb ground chicken
- 2 cloves garlic, minced
- 1 shallot, finely chopped
- 2 tablespoons soy sauce
- 1 tablespoon fish sauce
- 1 tablespoon oyster sauce
- 1 teaspoon sugar
- 1/2 teaspoon black pepper
- 1/4 cup breadcrumbs
- 1 egg
- 2 tablespoons fresh Thai basil leaves, chopped
- 2 tablespoons vegetable oil (for cooking)

For the Sauce:

- 2 tablespoons soy sauce
- 1 tablespoon oyster sauce
- 1 tablespoon fish sauce
- 1 teaspoon sugar
- 1 teaspoon sesame oil

For Serving:

- Fresh Thai basil leaves for garnish
- Cooked jasmine rice or noodles

Instructions:

Preheat Oven:
- Preheat the oven to 375°F (190°C).

Make the Meatball Mixture:
- In a large bowl, combine ground chicken, minced garlic, chopped shallot, soy sauce, fish sauce, oyster sauce, sugar, black pepper, breadcrumbs, egg, and chopped Thai basil leaves. Mix until well combined.

Form Meatballs:
- Shape the mixture into meatballs, about 1 to 1.5 inches in diameter.

Bake Meatballs:
- Place the meatballs on a baking sheet lined with parchment paper. Bake in the preheated oven for 15-20 minutes or until the meatballs are cooked through and golden brown.

Prepare the Sauce:
- In a small bowl, whisk together soy sauce, oyster sauce, fish sauce, sugar, and sesame oil to create the sauce.

Cook Meatballs in Sauce:
- Heat vegetable oil in a large skillet over medium heat. Add the baked meatballs to the skillet and pour the sauce over them. Cook for an additional 2-3 minutes, stirring gently to coat the meatballs in the sauce.

Serve:
- Serve the Thai Basil Chicken Meatballs over jasmine rice or noodles. Garnish with fresh Thai basil leaves.

Enjoy these Thai Basil Chicken Meatballs as a flavorful and aromatic dish. The combination of ground chicken, Thai basil, and savory sauces creates a delicious meal. Adjust the spice level and seasonings according to your preferences.

Thai Spicy Beef Salad (Nam Tok Nua)

Ingredients:

For the Beef:

- 1 lb (about 450g) flank steak or sirloin steak
- 2 tablespoons soy sauce
- 1 tablespoon fish sauce
- 1 tablespoon vegetable oil
- 1 teaspoon sugar
- Black pepper to taste

For the Salad:

- 1 red onion, thinly sliced
- 2-3 spring onions, chopped
- 1 cup cherry tomatoes, halved
- 1 cucumber, sliced
- Fresh cilantro leaves for garnish
- Fresh mint leaves for garnish

For the Dressing:

- 3 tablespoons lime juice
- 2 tablespoons fish sauce
- 1 tablespoon soy sauce
- 1 tablespoon roasted rice powder (available in Asian grocery stores) or rice flour
- 1 teaspoon sugar
- 1-2 Thai bird's eye chilies, finely chopped (adjust for spice preference)

Instructions:

Prepare the Beef:
- In a bowl, mix soy sauce, fish sauce, vegetable oil, sugar, and black pepper. Marinate the steak in this mixture for at least 30 minutes.

Grill or Sear the Beef:
- Grill the steak on a barbecue or sear it in a hot pan over medium-high heat. Cook to your desired doneness. Let it rest for a few minutes, then slice it thinly.

Make the Dressing:
- In a small bowl, whisk together lime juice, fish sauce, soy sauce, roasted rice powder (or rice flour), sugar, and chopped Thai bird's eye chilies.

Assemble the Salad:
- In a large bowl, combine the sliced beef with red onion, spring onions, cherry tomatoes, and cucumber.

Pour the Dressing:
- Pour the dressing over the salad and toss gently to coat everything in the dressing.

Garnish:
- Garnish the Thai Spicy Beef Salad with fresh cilantro leaves and mint leaves.

Serve:
- Serve the Nam Tok Nua immediately, either on its own or over a bed of lettuce. It's also commonly accompanied by sticky rice.

Enjoy the vibrant flavors of this Thai Spicy Beef Salad, where the tender beef is complemented by the zesty and spicy dressing. Adjust the level of spiciness by modifying the amount of Thai bird's eye chilies.

Thai Iced Coffee

Ingredients:

- 2 tablespoons coarsely ground coffee (dark roast preferred)
- 1-2 tablespoons sweetened condensed milk (adjust to taste)
- Ice cubes
- Water for brewing
- Optional: evaporated milk or regular milk for topping

Instructions:

Brew the Coffee:
- Brew strong coffee using your preferred method. You can use a French press, drip coffee maker, or any other method. Use about 2 tablespoons of coarsely ground coffee for every 6 ounces of water.

Sweeten with Condensed Milk:
- While the coffee is still hot, add sweetened condensed milk to your liking. Start with 1-2 tablespoons and adjust based on your preferred level of sweetness.

Mix Well:
- Stir the sweetened condensed milk into the hot coffee until well combined.

Cool the Coffee:
- Allow the coffee to cool to room temperature, then refrigerate it until chilled.

Serve over Ice:
- Fill a glass with ice cubes. Pour the chilled coffee over the ice.

Optional Milk Topping:
- For an extra creamy touch, you can add a splash of evaporated milk or regular milk on top of the iced coffee.

Enjoy:
- Stir the iced coffee, and enjoy your homemade Thai Iced Coffee!

Feel free to adjust the sweetness and milk ratios according to your taste preferences. Traditional Thai Iced Coffee is strong, sweet, and often enjoyed with a good amount of condensed milk. It's a perfect refreshing drink, especially on a hot day.

Green Curry Tofu

Ingredients:

For the Green Curry Sauce:

- 1 can (14 oz) coconut milk
- 2 tablespoons green curry paste
- 1 tablespoon soy sauce
- 1 tablespoon brown sugar
- 1 tablespoon fish sauce (or soy sauce for a vegetarian version)
- 1 lime, zest and juice
- 1 lemongrass stalk, bruised and chopped
- 2 kaffir lime leaves, torn into pieces (optional)
- 1 tablespoon vegetable oil

For the Tofu and Vegetables:

- 1 block (14 oz) extra-firm tofu, pressed and cubed
- 1 cup broccoli florets
- 1 bell pepper, sliced
- 1 carrot, sliced into thin strips
- 1 zucchini, sliced
- 1 cup snap peas, trimmed
- 2 tablespoons vegetable oil for stir-frying

For Garnish:

- Fresh basil leaves
- Thai bird's eye chilies, sliced (optional)
- Cooked jasmine rice for serving

Instructions:

Prepare Tofu:
- Press the tofu to remove excess water, then cut it into cubes.

Make Green Curry Sauce:
- In a large pan or wok, heat vegetable oil over medium heat. Add green curry paste and sauté for a minute until fragrant.

- Pour in coconut milk and stir well. Add soy sauce, brown sugar, fish sauce, lime zest, lime juice, lemongrass, and kaffir lime leaves. Simmer for 5-7 minutes, allowing the flavors to meld. Remove lemongrass and kaffir lime leaves.

Stir-Fry Tofu and Vegetables:
- In a separate pan, heat vegetable oil over medium-high heat. Add tofu cubes and stir-fry until golden brown on all sides. Remove tofu from the pan and set aside.
- In the same pan, stir-fry broccoli, bell pepper, carrot, zucchini, and snap peas until they are crisp-tender.

Combine Tofu, Vegetables, and Sauce:
- Add the stir-fried tofu to the pan with the vegetables. Pour the green curry sauce over the tofu and vegetables. Stir to combine and coat everything in the sauce.

Simmer:
- Allow the mixture to simmer for a few minutes until the tofu and vegetables are well coated and heated through.

Serve:
- Serve Green Curry Tofu over jasmine rice. Garnish with fresh basil leaves and sliced Thai bird's eye chilies if you like it spicy.

Enjoy this delicious and aromatic Green Curry Tofu as a satisfying and flavorful vegetarian meal. Adjust the level of spiciness by modifying the amount of green curry paste and Thai bird's eye chilies.

Thai Style Grilled Chicken Wings

Ingredients:

For the Marinade:

- 2 lbs chicken wings, split at joints, tips discarded
- 3 tablespoons fish sauce
- 2 tablespoons soy sauce
- 2 tablespoons oyster sauce
- 2 tablespoons honey or brown sugar
- 1 tablespoon minced garlic
- 1 tablespoon minced ginger
- 1 tablespoon sesame oil
- 1 teaspoon ground black pepper
- 1 teaspoon chili paste or Sriracha (adjust for spice preference)
- Zest and juice of 1 lime

For Garnish (Optional):

- Fresh cilantro, chopped
- Sesame seeds
- Lime wedges

Instructions:

Prepare the Marinade:
- In a bowl, combine fish sauce, soy sauce, oyster sauce, honey or brown sugar, minced garlic, minced ginger, sesame oil, ground black pepper, chili paste or Sriracha, and the zest and juice of one lime. Mix well.

Marinate the Chicken Wings:
- Place the chicken wings in a large zip-top bag or a shallow dish. Pour the marinade over the wings, ensuring they are well coated. Seal the bag or cover the dish and refrigerate for at least 2 hours, or preferably overnight, for the flavors to infuse.

Preheat the Grill:
- Preheat your grill to medium-high heat.

Grill the Chicken Wings:

- Remove the chicken wings from the marinade and let excess marinade drip off. Place the wings on the preheated grill. Grill for about 15-20 minutes, turning occasionally, until the wings are cooked through and have a nice char.

Garnish and Serve:
- Remove the grilled chicken wings from the grill and place them on a serving platter. Garnish with fresh cilantro, sesame seeds, and lime wedges if desired.

Serve Hot:
- Serve the Thai Style Grilled Chicken Wings hot as an appetizer or part of a delicious Thai-inspired meal.

These Thai Style Grilled Chicken Wings are a perfect combination of sweet, savory, and spicy flavors. Adjust the level of spice according to your preference, and enjoy them with the fresh and vibrant garnishes.

Pad Woon Sen (Stir-Fried Glass Noodles)

Ingredients:

- 200g glass noodles (cellophane noodles)
- 200g chicken, shrimp, or tofu (choose one or a combination)
- 2 tablespoons vegetable oil
- 2 cloves garlic, minced
- 1/2 cup onion, thinly sliced
- 1/2 cup carrots, julienned
- 1/2 cup bell peppers, thinly sliced (use a mix of colors)
- 1/2 cup cabbage, thinly sliced
- 1/2 cup mushrooms, sliced
- 2 eggs, lightly beaten
- 3 tablespoons soy sauce
- 1 tablespoon oyster sauce (optional)
- 1 tablespoon fish sauce
- 1 teaspoon sugar
- 1/2 teaspoon white pepper
- Green onions, chopped (for garnish)
- Lime wedges (for serving)

Instructions:

Prepare Glass Noodles:
- Soak the glass noodles in warm water for about 15-20 minutes or until they become soft. Drain and set aside.

Cook Protein:
- If using chicken or shrimp, cook them in a pan with a bit of oil until they are fully cooked. If using tofu, you can sauté it until golden brown. Set aside.

Stir-Fry Vegetables:
- In a wok or large pan, heat 2 tablespoons of vegetable oil over medium-high heat. Add minced garlic and sliced onions. Stir-fry for about 1-2 minutes until the onions are translucent.
- Add julienned carrots, sliced bell peppers, cabbage, and mushrooms. Stir-fry for another 2-3 minutes until the vegetables are slightly tender but still crisp.

Add Eggs and Noodles:

- Push the vegetables to one side of the pan and pour the beaten eggs into the other side. Scramble the eggs until they are just cooked.
- Add the soaked and drained glass noodles to the pan. Toss everything together to combine.

Season and Combine:
- Pour soy sauce, oyster sauce (if using), fish sauce, sugar, and white pepper over the noodles and vegetables. Mix well to ensure even coating.
- Add the cooked protein (chicken, shrimp, or tofu) back into the pan. Toss everything together until well combined and heated through.

Garnish and Serve:
- Garnish with chopped green onions. Serve Pad Woon Sen hot with lime wedges on the side.

Enjoy this tasty and satisfying Stir-Fried Glass Noodles as a flavorful Thai dish! Feel free to customize the vegetables and protein according to your preferences.

Thai Red Curry Mussels

Ingredients:

- 2 lbs fresh mussels, cleaned and debearded
- 1 can (14 oz) coconut milk
- 2 tablespoons red curry paste
- 1 tablespoon vegetable oil
- 1 red bell pepper, thinly sliced
- 1 onion, thinly sliced
- 3 cloves garlic, minced
- 1 tablespoon grated ginger
- 1 tablespoon fish sauce
- 1 tablespoon soy sauce
- 1 tablespoon brown sugar
- Juice of 1 lime
- Fresh cilantro leaves for garnish
- Thai basil leaves for garnish
- Red chili slices for garnish (optional)
- Cooked jasmine rice for serving

Instructions:

Clean Mussels:
- Scrub and clean the mussels under cold running water. Remove the beards and discard any mussels with broken shells or that do not close when tapped.

Prepare Ingredients:
- Slice the red bell pepper and onion thinly. Mince garlic and grate ginger.

Make Red Curry Sauce:
- In a large pot or wok, heat vegetable oil over medium heat. Add red curry paste and sauté for a minute until fragrant.
- Pour in the coconut milk and stir well to combine with the red curry paste.

Add Aromatics and Vegetables:
- Add minced garlic, grated ginger, sliced red bell pepper, and sliced onion to the pot. Cook for 2-3 minutes until the vegetables start to soften.

Cook Mussels:
- Add cleaned mussels to the pot. Stir to coat the mussels with the curry sauce.

- Cover the pot with a lid and simmer for about 5-7 minutes or until the mussels open. Discard any mussels that do not open.

Season the Dish:
- Stir in fish sauce, soy sauce, brown sugar, and lime juice. Adjust the seasoning to taste.

Garnish and Serve:
- Garnish the Thai Red Curry Mussels with fresh cilantro leaves, Thai basil leaves, and red chili slices if desired.
- Serve the mussels over cooked jasmine rice, ladling the delicious red curry sauce over the top.

Enjoy this Thai Red Curry Mussels dish, rich in flavor and with the perfect balance of spice and sweetness. It's a delightful seafood dish that can be enjoyed as a main course with rice or with crusty bread to soak up the flavorful broth.

Thai Pumpkin Custard (Sangkhaya Fakthong)

Ingredients:

- 2 cups pumpkin puree (from a small pumpkin)
- 1 cup coconut milk
- 1/2 cup palm sugar or brown sugar
- 4 eggs
- 1/2 teaspoon salt
- 1/2 teaspoon ground cinnamon (optional, for added flavor)
- 1/4 teaspoon ground nutmeg (optional, for added flavor)
- Banana leaves or parchment paper (for lining the mold)

Instructions:

Prepare the Pumpkin Puree:
- Peel and dice the pumpkin. Steam or boil the pumpkin until it's soft and easily mashed. Mash the cooked pumpkin to create a smooth puree. Allow it to cool.

Preheat the Oven:
- Preheat your oven to 350°F (180°C).

Prepare the Mold:
- Line a mold or baking dish with banana leaves or parchment paper. This adds a traditional touch and makes it easier to remove the custard after baking.

Make the Custard Mixture:
- In a mixing bowl, whisk together coconut milk, palm sugar or brown sugar, eggs, salt, ground cinnamon, and ground nutmeg. Whisk until the sugar is dissolved and the mixture is well combined.
- Add the pumpkin puree to the mixture and whisk until smooth and evenly blended.

Pour into Mold:
- Pour the custard mixture into the prepared mold.

Bake:
- Place the mold in the preheated oven and bake for approximately 45-50 minutes or until the custard is set. You can test the custard by inserting a toothpick into the center – it should come out clean when the custard is done.

Cool and Serve:

- Allow the Thai Pumpkin Custard to cool before slicing. It can be served warm or chilled.

Garnish (Optional):
- Garnish the custard with additional coconut milk or a sprinkle of toasted sesame seeds before serving.

Enjoy this Thai Pumpkin Custard as a delightful and comforting dessert. The combination of pumpkin, coconut milk, and warm spices creates a rich and flavorful treat.

Thai Mango Salad

Ingredients:

For the Salad:

- 2 ripe mangoes, peeled, pitted, and julienned
- 1 medium carrot, peeled and julienned
- 1 red bell pepper, thinly sliced
- 1/2 cup cherry tomatoes, halved
- 1/4 cup red onion, thinly sliced
- 1/4 cup fresh cilantro leaves, chopped
- 1/4 cup fresh mint leaves, chopped
- 1/4 cup roasted peanuts, chopped

For the Dressing:

- 3 tablespoons fish sauce
- 2 tablespoons lime juice
- 1 tablespoon soy sauce
- 1 tablespoon brown sugar
- 1-2 Thai bird's eye chilies, finely chopped (adjust for spice preference)
- 1 clove garlic, minced

Instructions:

Prepare the Mango and Vegetables:
- Peel, pit, and julienne the ripe mangoes. Peel and julienne the carrot. Thinly slice the red bell pepper, halve the cherry tomatoes, and thinly slice the red onion.

Make the Dressing:
- In a small bowl, whisk together fish sauce, lime juice, soy sauce, brown sugar, chopped Thai bird's eye chilies, and minced garlic. Adjust the sweetness and spiciness according to your taste.

Assemble the Salad:

- In a large bowl, combine the julienned mangoes, carrots, sliced red bell pepper, halved cherry tomatoes, sliced red onion, chopped cilantro, and chopped mint.

Add the Dressing:
- Pour the dressing over the salad ingredients.

Toss and Garnish:
- Gently toss the salad to ensure that all ingredients are well coated with the dressing.
- Sprinkle the chopped roasted peanuts over the top for added crunch.

Serve:
- Serve the Thai Mango Salad immediately as a refreshing side dish or as a light and healthy main course.

Enjoy this Thai Mango Salad with its vibrant colors and harmonious blend of sweet, savory, tangy, and spicy flavors. It's a perfect salad for warm weather and pairs well with grilled meats or seafood.

Chicken in Pandan Leaves (Gai Haw Bai Toey)

Ingredients:

- 1 lb chicken thighs, boneless and skinless, cut into bite-sized pieces
- 1 tablespoon oyster sauce
- 1 tablespoon soy sauce
- 1 tablespoon fish sauce
- 1 tablespoon sugar
- 1 teaspoon white pepper
- 2 cloves garlic, minced
- 1 tablespoon cilantro roots or stems, finely chopped (optional)
- Pandan leaves, cleaned and cut into 5-6 inch strips
- Vegetable oil for deep-frying

Instructions:

Marinate the Chicken:
- In a bowl, combine oyster sauce, soy sauce, fish sauce, sugar, white pepper, minced garlic, and chopped cilantro roots (if using). Mix well to create the marinade.
- Add the chicken pieces to the marinade, ensuring they are well coated. Let it marinate for at least 30 minutes, or preferably longer, in the refrigerator.

Prepare the Pandan Leaves:
- Clean the pandan leaves and cut them into strips of about 5-6 inches in length.

Wrap the Chicken:
- Take a piece of marinated chicken and wrap it in a strip of pandan leaf, securing it with a toothpick if necessary. Repeat for the remaining chicken pieces.

Deep-Fry the Chicken:
- Heat vegetable oil in a deep pan or wok over medium-high heat.
- Once the oil is hot, carefully add the pandan-wrapped chicken pieces, a few at a time, into the hot oil. Deep-fry until the chicken is golden brown and cooked through, about 5-7 minutes.
- Use a slotted spoon to remove the chicken from the oil and place them on a paper towel to drain any excess oil.

Serve:

- Serve the Chicken in Pandan Leaves hot, either on its own or with a dipping sauce of your choice.

Enjoy this aromatic and flavorful Thai dish of Chicken in Pandan Leaves. The pandan leaves infuse the chicken with a unique fragrance, making it a delightful appetizer or main course.

Thai Style Beef Jerky (Neua Dad Diew)

Ingredients:

- 1 lb beef sirloin or flank steak, thinly sliced against the grain
- 1/4 cup soy sauce
- 2 tablespoons oyster sauce
- 2 tablespoons fish sauce
- 2 tablespoons honey or brown sugar
- 1 tablespoon sesame oil
- 1 teaspoon ground coriander
- 1 teaspoon ground white pepper
- 1 teaspoon garlic powder
- 1 teaspoon onion powder
- 1/2 teaspoon five-spice powder
- 1/2 teaspoon dried chili flakes (adjust for spice preference)

Instructions:

Prepare the Marinade:
- In a bowl, combine soy sauce, oyster sauce, fish sauce, honey or brown sugar, sesame oil, ground coriander, ground white pepper, garlic powder, onion powder, five-spice powder, and dried chili flakes. Mix well until the sugar is dissolved.

Marinate the Beef:
- Add the thinly sliced beef to the marinade, ensuring that each slice is coated evenly. Cover the bowl and let it marinate in the refrigerator for at least 4 hours, or overnight for better flavor penetration.

Preheat the Oven or Dehydrator:
- Preheat your oven to its lowest setting (usually around 170°F or 75°C) or follow the instructions for your food dehydrator.

Drain Excess Marinade:
- Remove the marinated beef from the refrigerator and drain off any excess marinade.

Dry the Beef:
- If using an oven, place a wire rack on a baking sheet and arrange the marinated beef slices on the rack. Place the baking sheet in the preheated oven, leaving the oven door slightly ajar to allow moisture to escape. Dry the beef for 4-6 hours, or until it reaches your desired level of dryness.

- If using a dehydrator, arrange the beef slices on the dehydrator trays according to the manufacturer's instructions. Dry the beef for 4-6 hours or until it reaches the desired level of dryness.

Cool and Store:
- Allow the Thai Style Beef Jerky to cool completely before storing it in an airtight container. It can be kept at room temperature for a few days or refrigerated for longer shelf life.

Enjoy this Thai-style beef jerky as a tasty and protein-packed snack. Adjust the level of spiciness and sweetness in the marinade according to your taste preferences.

Thai Coconut Chicken Skewers

Ingredients:

For the Marinade:

- 1.5 lbs boneless, skinless chicken breasts or thighs, cut into strips
- 1 cup coconut milk
- 2 tablespoons red curry paste
- 2 tablespoons soy sauce
- 1 tablespoon fish sauce
- 2 tablespoons brown sugar
- 1 tablespoon lime juice
- 2 cloves garlic, minced
- 1 tablespoon lemongrass, finely chopped (optional)
- Wooden skewers, soaked in water for at least 30 minutes

For the Peanut Sauce (optional):

- 1/2 cup creamy peanut butter
- 1/4 cup coconut milk
- 2 tablespoons soy sauce
- 1 tablespoon brown sugar
- 1 tablespoon lime juice
- 1 teaspoon red curry paste
- Water (to adjust consistency)

Instructions:

Prepare the Marinade:
- In a bowl, whisk together coconut milk, red curry paste, soy sauce, fish sauce, brown sugar, lime juice, minced garlic, and lemongrass (if using).

Marinate the Chicken:
- Place the chicken strips in a shallow dish or a resealable plastic bag. Pour the marinade over the chicken, ensuring each strip is well coated. Marinate in the refrigerator for at least 2 hours, or overnight for more flavor.

Thread Chicken onto Skewers:

- Preheat your grill or grill pan to medium-high heat. Thread the marinated chicken strips onto the soaked wooden skewers.

Grill the Chicken:
- Grill the chicken skewers for about 6-8 minutes per side or until the chicken is fully cooked and has a nice char on the edges.

Prepare Peanut Sauce (Optional):
- In a small saucepan, combine peanut butter, coconut milk, soy sauce, brown sugar, lime juice, and red curry paste. Heat over low heat, stirring constantly until well combined and heated through. Add water to adjust the consistency if needed.

Serve:
- Serve the Thai Coconut Chicken Skewers hot, with or without the peanut sauce on the side.

Enjoy these Thai Coconut Chicken Skewers as a flavorful appetizer or main dish. The coconut-infused marinade adds a rich and aromatic flavor to the grilled chicken, making it a delicious and satisfying dish.

Pad Fak Thong (Stir-Fried Pumpkin)

Ingredients:

- 2 cups pumpkin, peeled and cut into bite-sized cubes
- 2 tablespoons vegetable oil
- 2 cloves garlic, minced
- 1 red chili, thinly sliced (optional, for heat)
- 1 tablespoon oyster sauce
- 1 tablespoon soy sauce
- 1 teaspoon fish sauce (optional, for added umami)
- 1 teaspoon sugar
- 1/4 cup water
- Fresh cilantro leaves for garnish

Instructions:

Prepare the Pumpkin:
- Peel the pumpkin and remove the seeds. Cut the pumpkin into bite-sized cubes.

Stir-Fry the Pumpkin:
- Heat vegetable oil in a wok or large pan over medium-high heat. Add minced garlic and sliced red chili (if using). Stir-fry for about 1 minute until fragrant.
- Add the pumpkin cubes to the wok. Stir-fry for another 3-4 minutes until the pumpkin begins to soften.

Make the Sauce:
- In a small bowl, mix together oyster sauce, soy sauce, fish sauce (if using), sugar, and water.

Cook the Pumpkin:
- Pour the sauce over the pumpkin in the wok. Stir well to coat the pumpkin cubes evenly with the sauce.
- Continue to stir-fry for an additional 5-7 minutes or until the pumpkin is fully cooked but still retains some firmness.

Garnish and Serve:
- Garnish the Stir-Fried Pumpkin with fresh cilantro leaves.
- Serve hot as a side dish or as a vegetarian main course with steamed rice.

This simple and flavorful Stir-Fried Pumpkin dish allows the natural sweetness of the pumpkin to shine. Adjust the level of spiciness and sweetness according to your taste preferences. It's a delightful and colorful addition to your Thai recipe repertoire.

Thai Rice Soup (Khao Tom)

Ingredients:

- 1 cup jasmine rice
- 6 cups chicken or vegetable broth
- 1 cup cooked chicken, shredded (optional)
- 2 cloves garlic, minced
- 1 tablespoon ginger, grated
- 2 green onions, sliced
- 1 tablespoon soy sauce
- 1 teaspoon sesame oil
- Salt and pepper to taste
- Fresh cilantro leaves for garnish
- Lime wedges for serving

Instructions:

Rinse and Cook the Rice:
- Rinse the jasmine rice under cold water until the water runs clear. In a pot, combine the rinsed rice and chicken or vegetable broth. Bring to a boil, then reduce the heat to low, cover, and simmer until the rice is cooked and has a porridge-like consistency.

Add Aromatics:
- In a separate pan, heat a bit of oil over medium heat. Add minced garlic and grated ginger. Sauté for a couple of minutes until fragrant.

Combine Rice and Aromatics:
- Add the sautéed garlic and ginger to the pot of cooking rice. Stir well to combine.

Season the Soup:
- Add soy sauce, sesame oil, salt, and pepper to taste. Adjust the seasoning as needed.

Add Cooked Chicken (Optional):
- If using cooked chicken, add shredded chicken to the soup and stir until heated through.

Garnish and Serve:
- Ladle the Thai Rice Soup into bowls. Garnish with sliced green onions and fresh cilantro leaves.

- Serve hot with lime wedges on the side. Squeeze lime juice into the soup before eating for an extra burst of flavor.

This Thai Rice Soup is a comforting and nourishing dish, and you can customize it by adding your choice of protein, vegetables, or herbs. It's a versatile recipe that can be adapted to suit your taste preferences.

Thai Shrimp Pancakes

Ingredients:

For the Shrimp Pancakes:

- 1 cup shrimp, peeled, deveined, and finely chopped
- 1 cup bean sprouts
- 1/2 cup green onions, finely chopped
- 1/4 cup cilantro, chopped
- 2 cloves garlic, minced
- 1 red chili, finely chopped (optional, for heat)
- 1 cup all-purpose flour
- 1 teaspoon baking powder
- 1/2 teaspoon salt
- 1/4 teaspoon black pepper
- 1 cup coconut milk
- Vegetable oil for frying

For the Dipping Sauce:

- 1/4 cup soy sauce
- 2 tablespoons rice vinegar
- 1 tablespoon honey or brown sugar
- 1 teaspoon sesame oil
- 1 teaspoon ginger, grated
- 1 green onion, finely chopped (for garnish)

Instructions:

Prepare the Dipping Sauce:
- In a small bowl, whisk together soy sauce, rice vinegar, honey or brown sugar, sesame oil, grated ginger, and chopped green onion. Set aside.

Make the Shrimp Pancake Batter:
- In a large mixing bowl, combine chopped shrimp, bean sprouts, chopped green onions, chopped cilantro, minced garlic, and chopped red chili (if using).

- In a separate bowl, whisk together all-purpose flour, baking powder, salt, and black pepper. Gradually add coconut milk to the dry ingredients, whisking continuously to avoid lumps.
- Pour the coconut milk mixture into the bowl with the shrimp and vegetables. Stir until well combined.

Fry the Shrimp Pancakes:
- Heat vegetable oil in a large skillet or pan over medium-high heat.
- Spoon the shrimp pancake batter into the hot oil, forming small pancakes. Cook for 2-3 minutes on each side, or until they are golden brown and cooked through.
- Remove the shrimp pancakes from the pan and place them on a plate lined with paper towels to absorb excess oil.

Serve:
- Arrange the Thai Shrimp Pancakes on a serving platter.
- Serve hot with the prepared dipping sauce on the side.

Enjoy these Thai Shrimp Pancakes with the savory shrimp and a hint of spice, complemented by the fresh flavors of bean sprouts and herbs. The dipping sauce adds a perfect balance of sweetness and tanginess to the dish.

Spicy Thai Pineapple Chicken

Ingredients:

- 1.5 lbs boneless, skinless chicken thighs or breasts, cut into bite-sized pieces
- 1 cup pineapple chunks (fresh or canned)
- 1 red bell pepper, sliced
- 1 onion, sliced
- 3 cloves garlic, minced
- 1 tablespoon ginger, grated
- 2 tablespoons vegetable oil
- 1/4 cup Thai red curry paste
- 1 can (14 oz) coconut milk
- 2 tablespoons fish sauce
- 1 tablespoon soy sauce
- 1 tablespoon brown sugar
- 1 teaspoon chili flakes (adjust to taste)
- Fresh cilantro leaves for garnish
- Cooked rice for serving

Instructions:

Prepare the Chicken:
- Cut the chicken into bite-sized pieces.

Cook the Chicken:
- In a large skillet or wok, heat vegetable oil over medium-high heat. Add minced garlic and grated ginger, sautéing until fragrant.
- Add the chicken pieces to the skillet and cook until browned on all sides.

Add Vegetables:
- Add sliced red bell pepper and onion to the skillet. Stir-fry for a few minutes until the vegetables start to soften.

Make the Sauce:
- Push the chicken and vegetables to one side of the skillet. Add Thai red curry paste to the other side and cook briefly until fragrant.
- Pour in coconut milk, fish sauce, soy sauce, brown sugar, and chili flakes. Stir well to combine the sauce with the chicken and vegetables.

Add Pineapple:
- Add pineapple chunks to the skillet. Simmer for 5-7 minutes until the chicken is cooked through, and the sauce has thickened slightly.

Adjust Seasoning:
- Taste and adjust the seasoning if needed, adding more fish sauce, soy sauce, or chili flakes according to your preference.

Garnish and Serve:
- Garnish the Spicy Thai Pineapple Chicken with fresh cilantro leaves.
- Serve hot over cooked rice.

Enjoy this Spicy Thai Pineapple Chicken with its perfect balance of sweet, spicy, and savory flavors. It's a delightful and colorful dish that's sure to please your taste buds.

Thai Coconut Tapioca Pudding

Ingredients:

For the Tapioca Pudding:

- 1/2 cup small tapioca pearls
- 2 cups coconut milk
- 1/2 cup sugar
- 1/4 teaspoon salt

For the Red Ruby (Tub Tim Krob):

- 1/2 cup water chestnuts, diced into small cubes
- Red food coloring
- 2 tablespoons tapioca flour
- 1/4 cup water
- Crushed ice (for serving)

For Coconut Syrup:

- 1/2 cup coconut milk
- 2 tablespoons sugar
- 1/4 teaspoon salt

Instructions:

Prepare Tapioca Pudding:
- Rinse the tapioca pearls under cold water. In a saucepan, combine the rinsed tapioca pearls, coconut milk, sugar, and salt. Let it soak for 30 minutes.
- After soaking, bring the mixture to a simmer over medium heat, stirring constantly. Reduce heat to low and simmer for an additional 10-15 minutes or until the tapioca pearls are translucent and the mixture has thickened. Remove from heat and let it cool.

Prepare Red Ruby (Tub Tim Krob):

- In a bowl, mix tapioca flour with water until well combined. In a separate bowl, toss diced water chestnuts with a few drops of red food coloring until they are evenly colored.
- Add the colored water chestnuts to the tapioca flour mixture. Stir until the water chestnuts are coated with the flour mixture.
- Bring a pot of water to boil. Add the coated water chestnuts to the boiling water. Cook until they float to the surface. Remove and rinse under cold water.

Make Coconut Syrup:
- In a small saucepan, heat coconut milk, sugar, and salt over medium heat. Stir until the sugar dissolves, and the mixture is heated through. Remove from heat and let it cool.

Assemble the Dessert:
- Spoon the prepared tapioca pudding into serving bowls.
- Add a generous amount of red ruby (colored water chestnuts) on top of the tapioca pudding.
- Drizzle the coconut syrup over the dessert.
- Serve with crushed ice for a refreshing touch.

Enjoy this Thai Coconut Tapioca Pudding, featuring the delightful combination of creamy coconut, chewy tapioca pearls, and vibrant red ruby water chestnuts. It's a cool and satisfying treat, especially on warm days.

Thai Basil Eggplant

Ingredients:

- 2 medium-sized eggplants, cut into bite-sized cubes
- 2 tablespoons vegetable oil
- 3 cloves garlic, minced
- 1 red chili, thinly sliced (adjust for spice preference)
- 1 lb ground chicken or pork (optional)
- 2 tablespoons oyster sauce
- 1 tablespoon soy sauce
- 1 teaspoon fish sauce
- 1 teaspoon sugar
- 1 cup Thai holy basil leaves (or regular basil if Thai basil is unavailable)
- Cooked jasmine rice for serving

Instructions:

Prepare the Eggplants:
- Cut the eggplants into bite-sized cubes. You can soak them in salted water for about 15 minutes to reduce bitterness, then drain and pat dry.

Stir-Fry the Eggplants:
- Heat vegetable oil in a wok or large pan over medium-high heat. Add minced garlic and sliced red chili. Stir-fry for about 30 seconds until fragrant.
- Add the eggplant cubes to the wok. Stir-fry for 5-7 minutes until the eggplants are tender and lightly browned.

Cook the Protein (Optional):
- If using ground chicken or pork, push the cooked eggplants to one side of the wok. Add the ground meat to the other side and cook until browned.

Combine and Season:
- Mix the cooked protein with the eggplants in the wok. Add oyster sauce, soy sauce, fish sauce, and sugar. Stir well to combine and coat the ingredients with the sauce.

Add Thai Basil:
- Once the eggplants and meat are coated in the sauce, add Thai holy basil leaves to the wok. Stir-fry for an additional 1-2 minutes until the basil leaves are wilted.

Serve:

- Serve the Thai Basil Eggplant over cooked jasmine rice.

Enjoy this flavorful and aromatic Thai Basil Eggplant as a delicious and satisfying meal. The combination of savory oyster sauce, soy sauce, and the fragrant Thai basil creates a delightful harmony of flavors.

Grilled Thai Lemongrass Chicken

Ingredients:

- 1.5 lbs boneless, skinless chicken thighs or breasts
- 3-4 stalks lemongrass, finely minced (white part only)
- 4 cloves garlic, minced
- 1 tablespoon fresh ginger, grated
- 2 tablespoons fish sauce
- 2 tablespoons soy sauce
- 2 tablespoons oyster sauce
- 1 tablespoon honey or brown sugar
- 1 tablespoon sesame oil
- 1 teaspoon ground coriander
- 1 teaspoon turmeric powder
- 1/2 teaspoon black pepper
- Lime wedges (for serving)

Instructions:

Prepare the Marinade:
- In a bowl, combine minced lemongrass, minced garlic, grated ginger, fish sauce, soy sauce, oyster sauce, honey or brown sugar, sesame oil, ground coriander, turmeric powder, and black pepper.

Marinate the Chicken:
- Cut the chicken into bite-sized pieces. Place the chicken in a bowl or resealable plastic bag. Pour the marinade over the chicken, ensuring that each piece is well coated. Marinate in the refrigerator for at least 2 hours, or preferably overnight for maximum flavor.

Skewer the Chicken:
- If using skewers, thread the marinated chicken onto skewers, leaving a little space between each piece.

Preheat the Grill:
- Preheat your grill to medium-high heat.

Grill the Chicken:
- Grill the lemongrass-marinated chicken skewers for about 6-8 minutes per side or until the chicken is fully cooked and has a nice char on the edges.

Serve:

- Remove the skewers from the grill and let them rest for a few minutes.
- Serve the Grilled Thai Lemongrass Chicken hot, garnished with lime wedges on the side.

Enjoy the aromatic and citrusy flavors of this Grilled Thai Lemongrass Chicken. It pairs well with steamed rice or a refreshing Thai salad for a complete meal.